LIVE A
LITTLE BETTER

LIVE A LITTLE BETTER

ONE MAN'S JOURNEY
OF SURVIVAL,
SOBRIETY, AND SUCCESS

JOHN BEYER

WITH GLENN PLASKIN

Worth

Published by Worth Books,
an imprint of Forefront Books, Nashville, Tennessee.

Distributed by Simon & Schuster.

Library of Congress Control Number: 2025909158

Print ISBN: 978-1-63763-401-1
E-book ISBN: 978-1-63763-402-8

Cover Design by Bruce Gore, Gore Studio, Inc.
Interior Design by Mary Susan Oleson, Blu Design Concepts

Printed in the United States of America

For Amy—Marrying you was the best "move" I ever made. With loving thanks for making every one of the dreams possible.

CONTENTS

PREFACE

MOVING THROUGH LIFE

I HAVE BEEN in the moving business for almost forty years. For me, moving is a metaphor for life.

I'm not sure when this first sunk in. I've done a lot of thinking about actually moving belongings from place to place and the concept of moving from one stage of life to another, moving forward and moving on.

When you pack up all your personal belongings—your furniture, all your *stuff*—and move to a new place, it is more than a mere change of location. You're changing *yourself*. You're starting all over again; the choices go beyond what items to take, what to discard. There is a duality of leaving things behind while also moving forward.

Whether you're moving three thousand miles to another town or just across the lobby, the process of dismantling one home and creating another is a gargantuan physical and emotional job.

I watched the faces of countless clients as the boxes were packed and then unpacked. I saw the fear and excitement caused by a big life move. I was witness to all the disruption and upheaval, all the uncertainty of starting over again—not to mention the second-guessing about how it will all turn out. The feelings of loss and sadness mixed with hope and optimism were always too big to fit in any boxes. Although I own a moving company, I see moving as more than a business. To me, moving represents the strong human need to change, to shed, and to grow. Moving creates forward motion that generates momentum and change.

When I was in my twenties and physically doing the moving jobs myself, I found out firsthand that moving was strenuous work. Most people watching movers do not fully appreciate the strength and endurance needed for twelve- to fifteen-hour days, or the planning required to get all the items packed and unpacked. There's a method to our madness as we wrap the furniture, stack the boxes, and plan the sequence of what comes out of the house to get loaded first, second, and last. Though it's not rocket science, it requires strategic planning and execution, just as does life.

I recall as the unloading of a truck progressed, I could start to see one or two more "tiers" before I got to the attic (the part of the truck that extends over the cab). I couldn't wait until I got there, because that meant it wouldn't be much longer until the job was all done.

When the last few pieces were finally brought into the new home, there was a huge sense of relief. Yet we were not yet 100 percent finished. There was still the assembly of tables, desks, beds, and dressers, more details, then you had to fold all the blankets, stack the dollies, and make the truck ready for the next move.

The work of being a mover is physically exhausting. There were jobs that never ever seemed to end. Even when it was getting dark and cold outside, and the skin on my hands would be cracking and bruised from gripping the wood furniture. Stopping was not an option, I had to keep going, giving up was never allowed. The next day my hands ached and my back burned, but those physical pains were eclipsed by the sense of accomplishment. Looking back, I now see each moving job was an exercise in the discipline of seeing something through from Point A to Point B, to the very end, no matter the challenges. The entire process was an example of perseverance.

Each of those thousand moves taught me not only how to start and complete things but also how to navigate the challenges, to pivot, and to always move forward. Each day and with every move, the job was never done until it was truly done.

In my personal and professional life, I've experienced many moves—life transitions that led me from place to place, or stage to stage, until I ultimately arrived to where I am today. There are some dark parts to my story—pervasive alcoholism being the overriding challenge I faced, in my parents' lives as well as my own. That does not make me special, because we all struggle with *something*. Life comes at us all. Each of us faces trials and tribulations, adversities and conquests. No one is exempt. To process what we experience and to "move on," we have to go *through* it, not *around* it.

My goal in sharing my journey is to shine a light on the human condition, to capture the raw pain and incredible strength that it takes to move through and move forward in each of our lives.

That's what moving is all about: tackling the unknown and moving forward. Even when we're disappointed or sad, we have to accept reality and move on. Moving is uncomfortable. It is unnerving. It is about change. But the change forces you to develop new habits, new friends, new relationships, and even new goals. It fosters growth. My experience taught me that moving isn't at all about reaching the destination. It's about what happens on the journey itself, which is often the more significant.

As you turn the page, I invite you to enter my world. Writing this book is not about detailing my accomplishments, although I have accomplished a lot, and you will see how I did it and why I was motivated to succeed financially. But my life is no longer about personal gain or material possessions. My burning desire is to leave a legacy of good works. I want to give back to society, to help others with little or less opportunity, and to help motivate them to move forward.

I want you, the reader, to experience what's happened to me during the last sixty-plus years. I hope you will gain something from reading the story of how I moved through life. As in every story, there are ups and downs, good luck and bad, disappointments and triumphs. There were some mornings when I woke up that I did not think that I would be able to move forward, but I did. I hope my journey will inspire you to move forward.

CHAPTER 1

MOVING APART

*I'll wait in this place . . . where
the shadows run from themselves.*

—"WHITE ROOM," CREAM (1968)

MOVING DAY was here.

Saturday, April 20, 1968, a date I will never forget. My first actual move. I was eight years old. That was the day my family moved from a luxury high-rise apartment building in the upscale Bronx suburb of Riverdale, New York, into a huge working-class housing complex fifteen miles away, in Queens.

Gone would be the full-time doorman and a white-gloved concierge—a uniformed attendant who held the door open for a kid like me as I got into the back seat of our family's Buick Electra 225. No more full-service deliveries and laundry pick-up and delivery downstairs, unless it was my mother.

On that spring day, instead of playing outside with my friends, I was inside our house, watching our furniture go out the door and into a moving truck. In retrospect, it was also my life as I knew it moving out that door, and I was moving into the unknown.

"Finish packing the boxes and close them up," my mom told me and my two older sisters, Denise, thirteen, and Cherie, eleven. All three of us were jolted by the emotions of this day. Denise and Cherie had close friends in their Riverdale school and didn't want to say goodbye. It was the same for me, torn away from my school and my old neighborhood. For the three of us, this was a move that meant leaving so much behind.

Moving is scary. It means change. It creates doubt. It can make you feel insecure. And, as I would later understand, when it comes to physical moves, you are either moving up in life or you are moving down. In our case, this was a move down.

Though unspoken, my sisters and I totally understood that this move was a fall from grace.

I asked myself over and over, *Why is this happening to us?*

I was a kid. I just didn't understand.

*   *   *   *   *

The events of April 20, 1968, were years in the making.

How Mom and Dad met had everything to do with their respective parents' immigration to the US. My maternal grandparents, Charles and Margaret Jessel, were French-born, raised in Alsace-Lorraine. They settled in Harlem in the early 1940s. Charles worked as a waiter and remained in the restaurant business for his entire life. (When he died, he got quite a write-up in the paper for being a famous waiter and a wine expert.)

Charles was an alcoholic. And from what I was told, he was physically abusive to my grandmother. (I never met either one of them, as they were long gone before I was born.) My mother—Germaine, nicknamed Gerry—told me her father used to physically hit her mother. Even more disturbing, he used to molest my mother's sister, Margaret.

Thinking of what my mother must have gone through with an abusive alcoholic father, I can imagine why she might have needed a way to numb herself with alcohol as an adult.

Coincidentally, my paternal grandparents, Andy and Mae Beyer, came from Alsace-Lorraine as well. Our family name, Beyer, was a common German name.

My grandfather, Andy Beyer, was a tall, hulky man who worked as a butcher. Nobody in the family talked a lot about him. There was something mysterious about it. I guess all families have these enigmas. In any case, I never met him. He died in his fifties of colon cancer.

The only grandparent I ever *did* know was my paternal grandmother, Mae (who looked quite German, with a Roman nose and icy steel-blue eyes). She was a stern, cold, and removed kind of woman, the mother of three: my dad, John George Beyer; his sister, Lynn; and his brother, Andy Jr. Mae was a distant mother except when it came to her absolute favorite child, my father. She idolized him and lavished him with affection. Just as on my mother's side, alcoholism was rampant in my father's family too. I don't know if my grandfather Andy drank much, and I know that Mae was not an alcoholic, but Andy Jr. became an alcoholic just like my dad. Andy's son (my first cousin) was also an alcoholic.

As fate would have it, when Andy and Mae Beyer migrated to the US, they moved onto the *same block* on 125th Street in Harlem as my mother's family. Like a storybook, my parents met at the corner candy store. It was kind of meant to be. They were in their late teens or early twenties at the time. I don't have a lot of details about how they met or their romance. That's the sad truth. I don't remember them ever talking to me about it. I recall having a sense that they were happy for those first years after they married and started having children in the mid-1950s, building a business and a family.

The early 1960s were good for my family. My dad was a very successful photographer. His company, Chester Studios—located in the Bronx, near our apartment—contracted to take the black-and-white school pictures for the entire New York City public school system. It was a monumental responsibility and a hugely lucrative account.

Dad was very gregarious, a *big* personality. When he walked into a room, people noticed him. He was about five feet eleven but looked even taller, with very broad shoulders, long arms, and piercing steel-blue eyes—a magnetic, confident presence. By the time he turned thirty he lost most of his hair, so he looked older than he actually was. But he was totally engaging, good-looking, and strong. And he had a vice grip handshake that never weakened. Even as he got older, he could still grab and crush my hand in a handshake. It was always intimidating, especially for his son.

When it came to my father, there was something all-knowing and wise about him and his demeanor. He had a command about him that I think, to some extent, I inherited. He was very smart and worldly, and he could converse about anything. If you wanted to fact-check something, you asked John Beyer. He read the paper and followed the news and was also a voracious reader. He would always have three or four novels going at the same time, with books strewn all over our house, the pages all flipped open, in various stages of completion. He took his knowledge out into the world and always seemed to be in command of the situation. He knew where he wanted to go and who he wanted to talk to.

With Dad's personality and skills as a photographer, Chester Studios was booming. When color photography was exploding in the sixties, Dad and his partner, Murray Rosenthal, invested too heavily in the all-new color-film processing machines. The stress caused by this investment would eventually take a toll on both my father and Murray, physically and financially. Taking pictures in color motivated the parents to buy more photos. Everyone was excited about this new color technology. The bright yellow-and-red Kodak logo is emblazoned in my memory forever.

Although my busy dad was doing well in business, he was not taking good care of himself. He was a heavy drinker and a chain smoker. Dad not only smoked cigarettes but also sat at home smoking Omega Little Cigars while he read. They were dirty and smelled awful. He also ate all the wrong foods—a steak-and-potatoes guy, living in the culture of the time. It was all about drinking and no exercise. Both Dad and Murray Rosenthal were overweight, particularly Murray—though he didn't drink heavily or smoke.

In 1965, both Murray and my dad suffered massive heart attacks that landed each of them in the intensive care unit of Montefiore Hospital. Dad was only forty-one at the time, and he was not expected to live. But after two long months in the hospital, Dad was released—weakened and depleted, but alive. Murray survived too. But Chester Studios did not.

As a result of their heart attacks, Dad and Murray could no longer meet the daily demands of running Chester Studios. The business was too big for them to manage, and they just couldn't do it anymore. I do not know why they did not try to sell it; all I remember is that one day it was there and one day it wasn't. Everything folded. My father was ultimately hired as an executive at Walker Color of New York, in Yonkers, another photography company.

Despite his heart attack and long hospitalization, Dad went right back to drinking, which further diminished his health. His heart muscle was so damaged that he was declared legally disabled. After his heart attack he received both Social Security disability and private disability insurance for the rest of his life. My father's weakened physical condition did not deter his drinking. Dad was a functional alcoholic, a daily drinker who could get through the day conscious and get back home in one piece.

Dad's heart attack was the beginning of the end not only of his business but of my parents' marriage as well. My mom was a striking woman. She was a very attractive redhead, bearing a resemblance to Lucille Ball. Lucy and Mom were both five foot seven. Lucy had blue eyes, but Mom had beautiful brown doe-like eyes, which I inherited from her. Mom did her hair up high in the popular bouffant style of the time and looked great when she was all dressed up. Dad loved having her on his arm. But she was no ornament. Mom was very bright; she had a sense of humor and could be very goofy at times.

My early childhood memories include Dad going out at night and wanting my Mom to go along with him. My mother was also a heavy drinker and a chain smoker too. But unlike Dad, Mom did not want to go out every night. She had the responsibility of being our primary parent. That did not stop her from drinking at home. Without Mom as his drinking companion, Dad looked elsewhere for company. I was very young, but I do remember there were numerous "girlfriends" and nights out when he didn't come home at all. I also remember how this hurt my mother and her being enraged by his disloyalty. This just made my mother drink more.

When Dad finally did come home, my sleep was interrupted by drunken brawls between my parents that went on into the early morning. As time went on these fights got worse and worse: clothing was tossed out windows, liquor bottles were broken, there were screams in the night, and the police were called, disturbing the calm luxury of our apartment building.

While these fights went on, my sisters and I huddled together, unable to sleep, scared by these violent arguments, wishing that they would end.

My parents' alcoholism was causing complete chaos in their lives and in ours. Neither of them had the capacity to get the help they needed. Worse than that, neither of them even recognized that they needed help.

My dad's heart attack, the loss of his business, and his diminished income compounded his stress, leading to even more drinking. It was a vicious cycle. The more he drank, the more his life became unmanageable. His tenure at Walker Color of New York came to an end too. The money dried up; my parents' marriage unraveled.

My parents legally separated. And that's when my mother, sisters, and I moved—without Dad—to LeFrak City.

In the 1960s, if you were driving along the Long Island Expressway, you could not miss the huge billboard advertising LeFrak City. The LeFrak slogan, "Live a Little Better," remained up on that sign for decades. As I said, LeFrak was a community intended primarily for working- and middle-class families who were interested in modern facilities but unable to afford Manhattan. Built in 1962 on forty acres of what was previously marshland, the community was the brainchild of New York real estate tycoon Samuel J. LeFrak.

Sam was a New York–born real estate developer with a reputation as a tough guy, and his company ranked forty-fifth on the *Forbes* list of the top five hundred private companies. There is no doubt that none of his millionaire friends would have wanted to live at the gargantuan cookie-cutter complex with 4,605 apartments, built alongside the Long Island Expressway in Corona, Queens, that we were moving into. Over fifteen thousand people lived there. It really was a city within a city, each of the buildings named after a country. Our building was called *The Panama*. And our apartment, 5M, was a two-bedroom, one-and-a-half bath unit. The best part of the apartment was the terrace, which became my regular refuge, a safe place where I could escape the insanity of my mother's drinking and listen to music on my black-and-gray Panasonic cassette radio. I would tune in to Cousin Brucie on 77 AM. And when a favorite song came on, like Stevie Wonder's "Superstition," I immediately pressed record. I always missed the first few bars of the song but tried my best to capture it. Music became my refuge, and I wanted to record my favorite songs so that I could listen to them when I needed them. Music was a source of comfort that I could rely on, unlike my parents.

My world was not confined to the terrace. Most of the time, just walking outside was an instant escape. To a kid, LeFrak City was like moving into a theme park. The complex was entirely self-contained, home to its own shops, including a beauty parlor and barbershop, a dry cleaner, a TV repair service, a drugstore, and a big luncheonette. The mall that housed all these amenities was the heart and soul of the community. The sheer scope of the place and the constant activity in it distracted me from the painful memory of moving.

LeFrak was like the day of the locust. There were people everywhere, and I mean everywhere—in the hallway, in the elevator, in the lobby, and of course in the mall. The playgrounds were packed. There were monkey bars and seesaws being used every day. It was really a kid's paradise, all of us running around the mall and outside in the parks, playing basketball, trading baseball cards, and playing ring-a-levio in the streets.

As much as I had been sad about leaving Riverdale, LeFrak turned out to be fun for me. I picked up a new passion, basketball. I spent hours dribbling the ball even in the rain. I got pretty good. The first friend I made was Alan Weinman, a lanky kid who was a decent athlete, a fellow basketball player. He lived in the building next door to us, called *U.S.* My second friend was Richie Weintraub, a very good-looking kid with a personality and a half. Richie was witty and smart, and people loved him. He lived just upstairs, in apartment 6C, with his mother, Elaine; his dad, Lenny; and his brother, Kenny.

Our moms got to know each other in *Le Girls*, the beauty parlor in the mall, which was always packed on Saturdays. Mom was a terrible binge drinker, and she could not hide this. The other women in the building, including Richie's mom, could see this. She could drink herself into a blackout or go extraordinarily long periods when she would literally stay drunk for weeks on end. These benders were marked by very few breaks from the bottle. When she drank, it wasn't pretty. Because she was unable to control her drinking, her habits were visible to everyone in the building. In addition to drinking, she smoked one cigarette after another, burning holes in pillows and mattresses, and also damaging the mahogany furniture in our apartment. There were times that she staggered into the lobby, completely drunk; she was routinely found on the floor of the elevator after falling down drunk. Everyone saw her in this condition—the security and maintenance staff, the neighbors, and my friends, including Richie and his mom. It was embarrassing and scary for me to see. Other times she would suddenly pull herself together and stop drinking for a while until she fell off the wagon again.

At the same time, Richie and I had become inseparable. We were both on the same Little League team and in the bowling league. We also played Wiffle ball outside in what was called the "red rink" playground. Right next to that rink were the basketball courts where we spent hours together shooting hoops.

Richie was my childhood best friend. We had many sleepovers: Richie's mother would invite me to stay at their apartment because his mom could see that things were unraveling in my household as my mother's drinking got worse and worse. It was evident to everyone in the building. Even if it wasn't so evident, it felt that way to me.

The biggest change for me after moving to LeFrak is that I didn't see my father very often. From the ages of eight to thirteen, my world consisted of my friends, mom, and two sisters. Dad just wasn't there. After we moved, Dad became a part-time bartender at the Midland Bar, located at the 179th Street subway, the last stop on the E and F trains in Jamaica, Queens, which then, was and still is at the crossroad where the socioeconomically diverse of New York City would convene in the same place to share a drink or a story. A left out of the bar took you to an area of mini-mansions that were the homes of the haves, and a right took you to an ethnically diverse neighborhood of small homes where the have-nots lived. The Midland was the meeting place that drew this diverse racial and economic crowd. There was a dynamic sense of community that brought everyone together, and it was the booze that held them there and kept them coming back, my dad included.

Dad had a side hustle as the neighborhood bookie working out of the Midland, making money as a bookmaker and small-time loan shark. While it was a big comedown from the days of owning his own photography business, Dad still controlled the room and commanded respect in this bar community. At the Midland, Dad was a big shot, a big fish in a very small pond. Everybody knew him. He was like the mayor in the bar, but as a father he was absent. Even when he was physically there for a quick visit to see us, he really wasn't present. I never felt that he truly wanted to spend much time with me or my sisters.

*   *   *   *   *

One day, after Dad started working at the Midland, much to my surprise, Mom announced, "Dad is going to take you to the Yankee game this Sunday. And he's picking you up at twelve, so be ready." I was ready at 11:00 a.m., baseball glove in hand, bouncing a baseball against the inside wall of the lobby.

Finally, I was going to be with my dad—at a Yankee game! I was super excited.

But noon came along, and Dad wasn't there yet. I strained my neck toward the street and thought to myself, *He'll be here soon.* At 12:15, I was still nervously bouncing the ball off the lobby wall, but there was no sign of Dad. I was getting anxious. I buzzed my mom on the intercom from the lobby, and as soon as she answered, I blurted out, "Did Dad call!?"

"Yes," she answered. "He's running late. He'll be here soon."

Ten minutes later, I buzzed her again. "Did Dad call back? Did he call!?"

"No, he didn't." Even at this age, I could hear Mom's voice changing.

I thought to myself, *We are going to miss the first inning.* I went back to the intercom and buzzed again. To this day I can clearly picture the old, aluminum metal frame of the intercom that was bent and decaying; our apartment number, 5M, was faded and almost worn off. The neglect was symbolic of the neglect that I was experiencing day in and day out.

At this point I was having a conversation with myself, *Should I buzz again? No, I'll wait.* But I was so impatient I buzzed anyway. This time it took longer for Mom to answer. In my head, I can still hear her slurred words. Without me even having to ask her anything, she uttered, "No, he didn't call." There was no need to say anything else. She just hung up.

I was crushed. By 1:30 I came to the realization that Dad might not be coming at all. But I waited anyway, holding on to a shred of hope. At 2:00, I buzzed up again. This time, no answer at all. I waited some more. I again stretched my neck to see the cars coming around the block. No sign of Dad.

Of course, he wasn't coming. He never even called. Eventually I went upstairs, seeking some comfort from my mom. But her eyes were only half open. She was totally drunk. I grabbed my Panasonic cassette radio and went onto the terrace, which didn't have much of a view, as it faced the parking lot. I heard the announcer shout as Yankees outfielder great Roy White stole home. I listened to the game as tears poured down my face, thinking, *I'm supposed to* be *there, in the stands with my dad, watching this happen.* To say I was disappointed is an understatement. I was devastated. I felt invisible. And I didn't have anyone to tell.

After my father's disappearing act, I didn't hear from him for a week. When he finally called, he made a lame excuse, just a passing remark, like, "Something came up." Then he changed the subject. Unfortunately, this would not be the first or the last time Dad would make a promise and break it.

*   *   *   *   *

If the story about waiting for Dad taught me anything, it taught me that I had to rely totally on myself. I could not count on him. On the Monday morning after that baseball game fiasco, with my mother hungover and asleep, I got myself ready for school, ate some cereal, and tried to shake off the terrible weekend. However, there was no moving on from my bad weekend. When I opened my front door, things only got worse. I found an eviction notice plastered to our door. It wasn't the first time. With both parents being alcoholics, and neither one pulling in a reliable income, we were going to be thrown out of our apartment yet again.

At this point, Dad was broke, living with his mother seven miles away in Jamaica, Queens. I never knew how much rent he was paying her, but I'm certain it was a lot less than the $238 a month we were paying LeFrak. Needless to say, his financial support was nonexistent. Of course, according to the separation agreement, he was supposed to pay child support, but he wasn't sending the money. We had to depend on Mom's income whenever she *could* work, which all depended on how much she was drinking.

Her boss, Diane von Furstenberg, a Belgian fashion designer who rose to prominence in the sixties and seventies, took a genuine liking to Mom and cared enough about her to get her some help. Diane knew that Mom was a drinker. When Mom was on a bender and couldn't function at work, Diane would send her to a rehab for a month or two to dry out. While Mom was gone, my sisters were thrust into the role of parents, looking after me, at about ten, and themselves. Then, when our mother got sober, she'd go back to work again. This went on for years, back and forth between clean periods and blackouts. Ultimately, because she couldn't hold down a full-time job, she wound up working as a temporary secretary for Kelly Girls. It didn't pay great, but it was better than nothing and made it possible for her to work between drinking binges.

Mom was wonderful when she was sober. She reminded us to do our homework assignments. She would make breakfast. And she always pressed my shirts and made sure I combed my hair and brushed my teeth and looked good. And if I had to go to the doctor, she took me.

When she was good, she was really good. In fact, when Mom wasn't drinking, she was lighthearted and really very funny. She made corny jokes and lightened every room that she walked in, the life of the party. She could become hysterical with laughter, but you never knew how long it would last. From my observation, I would say her personality was a little bipolar, with huge mood swings. She was erratic and often withdrew from reality. She was either drunk—completely absent emotionally and devoid of any ability to function—or she was sober and behaved like a true mom. Unfortunately, her sobriety did not hold, and she inevitably started drinking again, and when she did, she neglected the responsibilities of being a mother.

Mom's erratic behavior resulted in an inconsistent and unreliable flow of money. She was always behind on the rent and the bills, so the eviction notices started to pile up almost upon moving into LeFrak. It became routine. Month after month we were late with our rent. In fact, the US marshals would sometimes knock on our door, threatening to move our things into the street.

On several occasions, we were so many months behind that the movers *did* move our things into the hallway. I have a vivid memory of my drunk mom holding her housedress closed with one hand, smoking a cigarette, and drinking vodka as a US marshal tried to sneak a peek at her nude body underneath. There we were, waiting for *someone* to show up with the money. On that day, Grandma Mae came through with the $238. Richie gave a deep sigh of relief when he saw our furniture being moved back into the apartment. He desperately wanted me to stay. I couldn't help but wonder: Who was going to take care of me?

Because Mom was frequently drunk or hungover, she couldn't help me get ready for school, make breakfast, or pack a lunch, much less clean the apartment. That role fell to my sisters, Denise and Cherie. They loved their little brother and were very protective of me.

Both my sisters were beautiful. Denise had full, perky lips, a cute smile, and a great figure (frankly, *a great ass* is the only way to put it). With her long, flowing brown hair and sparkling green eyes, she was very sexy. The teenage boys obviously liked her. But she was popular with everyone and had a lot of friends. Part of her appeal was that she was confident, extroverted, and assertive, edgy in that she didn't take any crap from anybody. She could be intimidating. You knew that she was becoming a very confident young woman. As the eldest (who had to deal with an alcoholic mother and an absentee-alcoholic father), being assertive was a protective system, both for herself and for Cherie and me.

Cherie was also very pretty, with dark brown hair and beautiful deep blue eyes. But she was a little bit quieter, more reserved and introverted than Denise. She had boyfriends and plenty of friends too. But unlike Denise, Cherie struggled a bit in school. Admittedly, *none* of us took school very seriously. Neither my mother nor father offered any supervision, encouragement, discipline, or structure. Also, once we were past age twelve, we all worked. Both my sisters worked in the dry cleaner downstairs in the mall. In fact, when it came to work, Cherie was very strong-minded in her own way and wanted to become independent as soon as she could. On the brink of her sixteenth birthday, she saved up all her money, and as soon as she was able to drive, she bought herself a used red Plymouth Barracuda. It was exceptionally cool. She became our mode of transportation. So even though she was quiet, she was a go-getter and was far better at planning than either me or Denise.

I watched my sisters do the best that they could to find their way through adolescence while dealing with all the pain and insanity of our household. As I said, they became my surrogate parents, and I felt protected by them when I needed it. While on one level LeFrak was an oasis, on another level there was significant racial tension and tremendous drug use, including many heroin-related deaths.

I remember one time I accidentally hit a kid in the face with a Wiffle Ball bat and I thought that kid he was going to kill me. Cherie stepped right in and made it all go away. Cherie protected me several times. Other teenagers were *not* easily going to intimidate or threaten any of the three of us.

Denise was even more intimidating. One day Cherie herself was being bullied by a beautiful girl whose name also happened to be Denise. Our Denise stepped in and had a fistfight with her, right in the middle of the LeFrak mall. She clocked that girl in the nose. She hit her so hard that the girl was choking on her own blood. This was in front of hundreds of people. The fight echoed through the entire complex. After that, nobody ever messed with my sisters or me again. All the girls were afraid of them.

At home, my sisters could be just as combative with my mom. When my mother was frustrated, angry, or drunk, she regularly screamed and yelled at my sisters and would chase them around the dining room table. I remember her once pinning my sisters down on the floor and smacking them. The reason for doing so was usually something inane like cleaning their room or doing their homework.

During these battles, I imagined that Mom was attempting to parent us. She was trying to get it together and discipline us and exert her authority. But she certainly was not going about it the right way. She didn't have the coping skills to handle three kids on her own. My mom told me that she felt abandoned by our father, both financially and emotionally. It was clear that as the only parent, she was overwhelmed, at the end of her rope. My sisters acted out their frustration and pushed the envelope. They were rebelling because they didn't respect anything Mom said *because* she was a drunk. And then the arguments would escalate and would get physical. LeFrak became a scary place, where even people's shadows ran from themselves.

Both my sisters escaped our apartment as early as they could. By age fourteen or fifteen, Denise moved from couch to couch at her friends' houses while Cherie moved in with my grandmother, Mae. I was left alone with my mother to fend for myself. I felt more alone than ever. At one point, one of our neighbors, we never found out who, called child protective services, telling them that I was being abused. Upon reflection, I wasn't abused, I was neglected. Sometimes there was nothing in the refrigerator but mayonnaise; old, packaged cheese; and bread. If the bread wasn't moldy, I was very happy that I could make a cheese-and-mayonnaise sandwich with it. At other times, I lived on Swanson TV dinners—when we could afford them. But no matter what, I had holes in my sneakers and my pants were too short.

At age eleven, I realized that if I literally wanted to *eat*, I was going to have to earn my own money.

CHAPTER 2

THE FIRST OF MANY

How can you help it when the music starts to play,
and your ability to reason is swept away?

—"EVERYBODY PLAYS THE FOOL,"
THE MAIN INGREDIENT (1972)

ONE DAY, when I was about eleven years old, and very hungry, I walked across the street from our apartment to our local Waldbaum's grocery store. I started helping people carry their groceries—usually either older women or young moms with children. I'd lift their bags out of the shopping carts and carry them over to their cars, and then load them in the trunk. Sometimes they would tip me a quarter! I loved it and would be waiting for the next person to come out of the store before the last car was out of the parking lot.

I noticed that the stray shopping carts made it difficult for people to pull in and out of the lot. I would collect the errant carts and put them back in a line, arranging them in an orderly long row. Then I would pick up a broom and start sweeping the parking lot. The second time I did this, the manager came out of the store and walked right up to me.

"What are you doing, kid?" he roughly asked. I assumed that he was going to throw me off the property.

"I'm just here to make some money," I told him quietly, "and help people put their groceries into their cars for tips." Would you believe that at the end of the day he handed me $2.00. And he thanked me. I realized in that moment that I had created my first job. It felt incredible. This was a turning point in my life. It was empowering. And so began my relationship with money.

After that, I went back to the grocery store parking lot as often as I could. Eventually, I started a different job. My success in the parking lot gave me the self-esteem to walk into our local pizza shop, called the Pizza Nosh. I saw guys delivering pizza who weren't much older than me. I remember thinking, *Why couldn't I do it?* But the manager looked at me (skinny and young) with skepticism: "Do you think you can ride this bike?" he asked, pointing to a big red Schwinn, a heavy steel bike with large, sealed metal boxes on it. I nodded my head yes. And that was it. I got the job. I admit it was very difficult riding that huge bike with pizzas and soda bottles loaded onto it. But I did it.

The good thing about working at the Pizza Nosh was that I was allowed a free slice of pizza on my shift, which was a lot better than a Swanson TV dinner. As I started to earn money, I appreciated the freedom that came with that and the ability to not settle but rather have what I wanted. In this case, I wanted a veal parmesan hero. And I remember Vinny, the owner, saying, "You snob, you little brat. You want a *veal* parmesan hero?! Who the hell do you think you are, John Beyer?" But I wanted it. I now could pay the extra dollar he was charging me for it, so I could have my veal parmesan hero instead of the slice. That's who I was from the beginning. I always wanted to have what I wanted and would find a way to get it. I'm still that way to this day. If somebody tells me I can't have it, I will insist on getting it.

At age twelve, I also began working at Sherwood Drugs on Saturday afternoons. I got the job by walking in and asking for it. I told the owner, "I can stock the shelves and I can do deliveries for you." I must have made a good impression. I was clean-cut and presentable and made sure to comb my hair. They gave me the job for Saturday afternoons. Then for Sundays, I got what would become my most profitable job, working at the super-busy luncheonette in LeFrak. It was like Grand Central Station, a bustling business located right in the hub of the entire complex with seemingly thousands of people in and out during the day. My job there was washing dishes, doing deliveries, and putting the Sunday newspapers together. After all the newspapers were piled up, they were actually taller than my own height at the time. I then did deliveries. I worked fourteen or sixteen hours a day, and by the end of my shift I was too exhausted to even move the wet mop across the floor.

Although it was a lot of hard work, I felt proud that I had these three jobs—delivering pizzas a few nights a week, working at the drugstore on Saturdays, and working all day long at the luncheonette on Sundays. The three jobs together yielded me $125 a week. For a twelve-year-old in 1972, that was a fortune.

In addition to my three jobs, I also started traveling to my father's bar, the Midland, in order to earn an allowance and get attention from him. It would take me forty-five minutes and two trains to get from my apartment to the bar. When I arrived, my dad would tell me to bring all the beer up from the basement and stock the shelves. I learned how to tap a beer keg when I was thirteen. On my break, I would sit there at the bar and drink Coca-Colas with cherries in them. But by the time I was fifteen or sixteen I was allowed to have a little glass of beer—which made me feel more adult and gave me a little buzz. This bar would become a monumental part of my life. The people I drank with and knew there became like a second family to me, including the bartenders and customers. Eventually I would truly come to know and love many of them.

All these jobs combined kept me busy and gave me enough money to finally buy a decent pair of sneakers without holes in them! Before that, I would have to line the bottoms of my worn-out sneakers with baseball cards in order to cover the holes and protect me from water seeping in and from my foot scraping up against the rough asphalt.

How did I get the baseball cards? All the guys at LeFrak would *flip* (trade) them. I hardly had any to flip, but sometimes they would have throwaways, doubles. And they would just drop them on the ground. I would sneak the throwaways and put them in my pocket, secretly using them to line my sneakers. I was embarrassed for them to know what I was doing. It was embarrassing and kind of sad.

As I remember it, back in the seventies the white guys at LeFrak wore Converse sneakers, and the black guys wore Pro-Keds. By this point, the neighborhood was more black than white, and racial tensions were high. More than once, two or three of the new guys pushed me up against an elevator and rifled through my pockets for loose change. I earned respect by getting good at basketball. It was a survival tool. In fact, once I got really good, the guys who had roughed me up picked me to play on their teams instead of robbing me.

* * * * *

My move from childhood to adolescence coincided with my earning money. I began to feel more and more grown up. Adolescence is a time of *firsts*: body changes, rebellious behavior, and newfound independence. For me, my personal rebellion meant cutting classes. Puberty was also the first time I drank and thought about my virginity and how to lose it.

When I was thirteen, I met a beautiful girl named Laura, who looked a lot like a young Natalie Wood. At the time, she was twelve and incredibly mature looking for her age, having fully blossomed already. She had dark hair and big, beautiful brown eyes. She came from a troubled family with a father who was pretty rough and abusive to her and to her two sisters. Personality-wise, she was sarcastic and witty, though not particularly extroverted. She moved with quiet confidence. She was not a good student or great at sports, but Laura had other attributes that turned heads in the neighborhood.

All the guys in school, including my good friend Richie Weintraub, were in competition, vying for her attention, wanting to get to know her better. But I was the lucky one who managed to "*get* her."

It all started with me hanging out in the hallway, then carrying her books on the way home from school. Like me, Laura had no supervision at home, so we were spending a lot of time together there. Sometimes she would invite me into her apartment, or I'd go along with her on a regular babysitting job in the same building. I remember so well laying with Laura on this white shag carpet while listening to the Al Green song "Let's Stay Together." I lost my virginity on that carpet. I was young and inexperienced, and it was over rather quickly! And right afterward, I remember being panicked about her getting pregnant, which she didn't. We were very grateful.

Although we were discovering each other sexually, that wasn't the main focus of our relationship. It was more than that: Because the two of us had such horrible home environments, we were truly seeking each other to find *solace*. And being together in that apartment felt like a place of refuge. It was comforting. It was a place to go where we could listen to music and be alone. We were safe.

We dated for a year and a half, until her family moved away

when she was fourteen. But we stayed connected for years after that, even though our relationship didn't last beyond middle school.

It was also around this time that I had my first drink with my best buddies, Richie and Jeff. We were always super competitive about everything—sports, girls, and now drinking! The first few times we managed to get some beer, we drank in a staircase hidden away in one of the towers at LeFrak. We were "shot-gunning" the beer by punching a hole in the can near the bottom, then placing our mouths over the hole and pulling the tab on the top, all at the same time. This created a vacuum, and the beer gushed out, the liquid rushing down our throats.

Shot-gunning was one way to get buzzed very quickly. We guzzled down three cans in a row. I was the one who didn't spill any. While the other guys spilled beer all over the place, I tried to *catch* what they were spilling with my hands and drink it, not wanting to waste a drop. Many times while we were laughing and having a great time, I would say, "Let's go get some tall boys," which were sixteen-ounce cans of beer rather than twelve-ounce cans. Being underage was no deterrent to get beer. One way I got beer was to steal it at the drugstore where I worked. Other times, we would pay some of the older kids to go into the deli to get it for us.

When I turned fifteen or sixteen, the drinking age was only eighteen, but I could get away with buying the beer myself since I was tall and looked older than my age.

I remember two things about my first experience with alcohol: My body felt warm, and I immediately wanted *more* . . .

and more. Among my friends, I drank differently than anybody else; I always consumed the most alcohol and I always wanted more. To me, getting drunk was liberating. I felt invincible and so much looser and uninhibited than being sober. It was an incredible feeling, especially when you're a kid.

Even though my mother was constantly drinking, she would have totally disapproved of it for me. I had to keep it a secret. When she was aware of my drinking beer, she attempted to ground me. But it never stuck. My mother was either not home or drinking herself—there was no way that she was going to supervise me; I just did what I wanted to do.

One time, when I was thirteen, I scored a bottle of MD 20/20, nicknamed Mad Dog. It's a cheap wine made from citrus fruits with artificial flavor and color. Artificial everything. It's disgusting alcohol that probably should be banned. And I somehow got ahold of it. I don't remember how. I drank the entire bottle myself and got very sick. I remember throwing up all over my sneakers, which really bothered me for two reasons: One, my mother was most likely going to see it, and two, I had wrecked my precious Pro-Keds, which I had worked so hard to buy. I remember trying to clean up those sneakers the best that I could. But that was one of the few times I ever really got sick from alcohol. I never drank Mad Dog 20/20 again, but, just like my mother and father, I went on to drink other stuff.

Drinking was not my only issue. I was becoming a delinquent, a rebel, and a criminal. When I was about fourteen years old, still living in LeFrak, I was approached by a twenty- year-old gang member who made me commit crimes. It was not my idea. But he was huge, a monster, a very intimidating guy who was older than me and scared the shit out of me. He forced me into helping him commit armed robberies inside the elevators at LeFrak City by threatening to beat me up if I didn't. Here's how we did it: He had a guy inside the elevator pretending to be a passenger. My job was riding on top of the elevator holding a gun. An unsuspecting woman would enter the elevator, and I would stop the elevator in between floors. The guy planted in the elevator would also pretend to be a victim as well. I would open the hatch and point the gun down at her and say, "Just hand him your wallet and your pocketbook." After the victim complied, I would take off and release the elevator. The guy inside would pry open the doors and jump out. He would say, "I'll call security," but of course he never would. This would give him enough time to get away while the other person was trapped in the elevator. I knew that I was doing the wrong thing, this was not me, but I was just too scared not to comply with his demands given his threats.

Then one day, the big intimidating guy just disappeared. I felt relief that I could now move on from this stage of my life that I felt badly about. Even though he was gone, I was still acting out as a rebel and no one could tell me what to do, especially my parents.

Neither I nor my sisters had any respect for either of our parents, which made it impossible for either of them to discipline or guide us. Up until I was thirteen, I was a model student, smart and conscientious, placed in all accelerated classes and motivated. And I looked the part: Starting when we lived in Riverdale and I was attending Catholic school, I was always dressed as neat as a pin. One day as a grade-school kid, the principal at St. Gabriel's, Sister Rose, came into our classroom. Everybody was petrified of her. And pointing to me, she said to my teacher, "I'll see that boy now." I was panicked. I had to stand up. And she walked me down the hall and took me into an eighth-grade classroom. Here I was in the second grade and I'm in front of all the eighth graders who had just gotten back after recess. Looking me up and down, she made me an example of how my shirt was still tucked in and my tie was still straight, unlike the other kids, who were a mess after recess.

I consistently ranked in the top five students in my class, but with the advent of my drinking and foray into crime came a corresponding deterioration in my mindset. I stopped working, but more disturbing, I stopped caring. For me, this was my first experience in downward or backward moves.

When I was in seventh grade, I was doing so well academically that I was supposed to skip the eighth grade entirely and move right on to ninth. But by the time I was thirteen going on fourteen, I stopped studying and my grades immediately dropped. I was becoming more rebellious, no longer the good little boy getting great grades and doing my homework. I went from being goody two shoes, following the rules, to being *Rebel Without a Cause*. (I was like the guys in the film, one of those emotionally confused teenagers quickly becoming a delinquent.) I just didn't care anymore. As I look back on it, I view the change in my behavior as a result of both the natural rebelliousness of adolescence and that complete lack of supervision and account-ability at home. It was a cry for attention as well.

Obviously, I had no incentive to study. So, toward the end of seventh grade, with my grades in a free fall, including a failing grade in math, my guidance counselor told me, "John, if you fail math, you're not going to skip eighth grade and go to high school early." I had an attitude like, *So what?*

On the day my counselor told me I would *not* be skipping eighth grade, I was disappointed. But he told me that I could still take accelerated classes just as I did before. I was not interested. I thought to myself, *If I'm not gonna skip, then why should I be taking accelerated classes? Why should I work so hard?*

I told the counselor, "Take me out of all the accelerated classes."

"John," he warned me, "don't do that."

We came to a compromise. I managed to get him to take me out of the accelerated science, math, and social studies classes. The only accelerated class I kept was English, which was my favorite subject. I was always good in it, and I liked to write both essays and poetry. But I remember going into eighth grade in the less advanced classes and feeling out of place, like I didn't belong there. The curriculum was below my capacities, so I just blew off my classes. It's amazing I didn't pursue a life of crime.

Even though my interest in academics was waning, I remained a very good athlete—basketball and swimming were my two best sports. And I was disciplined about it. On the swim-ming team, I was one of the better backstrokers. And there was no problem finding a place to swim in LeFrak. Swimming was solitude. I liked the quiet of it—there was just something peaceful about it.

In addition to athletics, I also loved singing. I always had a good voice. I was encouraged to sing from the time I was ten. My mother would turn on the record player with one of her two favorites, either Andy Williams or Frank Sinatra. She would tell me to stand there and sing along to the records. I loved it because this was one way I was getting attention from my mother. I could sing on pitch and was pretty good, which led to a role in the chorus at school and also participating in concerts.

I recall as early as the fifth grade, Richie Weintraub and I sang "Joy to the World" by Three Dog Night at a school concert. There we were, singing in front of everybody in this big auditorium. I liked the attention. And by the time I was in the eighth grade, I had performed a number of songs, including "Colour My World" by Chicago, in front of the whole school. I discovered that singing in front of everybody in the auditorium made you popular! I won the chorus award in middle school. And that was when my music teacher pushed me to audition for the renowned and very selective High School of Music & Art. Since I sang all the time, I thought, *Why not try?*

At thirteen, I went to the audition by myself. I had to take four different trains to get to Morningside Drive and 135th Street in Harlem, where the school is located. I walked up the stairs of that school and I sang two songs, "Raindrops Keep Fallin' on My Head" and "On a Clear Day," and I got in! To this day I'm proud of that accomplishment. And I think my mother was happy because she always loved music and always wanted me to sing for her. Unfortunately, the timing wasn't right because it was around this time of my life that I started to move away from myself and into darker spaces. I started school but I hated it. I made no friends there and I dreaded the four-train commute from LeFrak. It was horrible. Two hours of travel back and forth every day. I quit after three months. I hadn't learned the lessons of moving and the ability to persevere until the end. It didn't help that my parents were indifferent to my quitting. Their attitude was, "Do whatever you want. If that's what you think best, do it." And that is what I did.

On my own, at no more than fourteen, I decided to transfer to the school where some of my friends were going—John Bowne High School, located in Flushing, Queens. It was a huge school with nearly four thousand students. I was bused from LeFrak into Flushing. But by the time I started at John Bowne, it was already late October or early November. Walking in as the newcomer made me feel disoriented, self-conscious, and uncomfortable, like a stranger in a strange land. The consequence of this choice was that I just cut classes more and more often.

When I cut class, I met up with the LeFrak boys who were also cutting classes. We went to see Tony the Barber, who owned a little rinky-dink three-chair shop across the street from LeFrak, on the same block as the Pizza Nosh and Sherwood Drugs. Tony allowed all of us young guys to skip class and hang out in the back of his barbershop, which became a haven for us.

We drank beer and played card games like Knock Rummy for money. My crew consisted of my buddies Richie, Jeff, and Steve, and Tony was our enabler and a bad influence.

This hanging out phase continued through my freshman year of high school. I cut class the entire year. I didn't go to school. Overnight, I went from being in all accelerated classes and getting A's, to the High School of Music & Art, to a high school dropout. This all happened in 1974. It was a disaster. A year of backward movement.

My life was in shambles. I was a mess. I even lost the support of my sisters, who were doing their own thing and trying to find their own way through life. I was lost and terribly alone and, just like my parents, unaware that I needed help.

At some point, I do not remember the when or why of it, my sister Denise learned what was going on and found me.

"What the hell are you *doing*?" she yelled. Once Denise knew, Cherie knew. I don't know if one of them told Dad, but one day he made a very rare appearance and just showed up outside the barbershop to confront me. When I realized he was there, I took off and headed up the street and kept my distance as my dad followed me down the block. At fourteen, I was fast enough to easily get away from him since he was not in good shape. But his mere appearance startled and stopped me. In a low and threatening tone, he said, "If you don't go back to school, you're going to be in big trouble, and you will regret it."

Dad's presence both scared and impressed me. I guess I liked the attention from him, even if he was angry. After all, he didn't show up very much. And his presence demonstrated that he cared. I liked the very unusual attention.

As a result, I went back to school. I enrolled and attended summer school in the summer of 1975. I had to take summer school classes. The guidance counselor told me, "If you don't agree to go, we are never letting you back in the building."

I didn't know if that threat was true or not—but I took it seriously. It actually scared me, because I wanted the option of being *able* to return to school if and when I wanted to. What was I going to do if I didn't go to school?

So even though part of me didn't believe Dad's threat, I thought, *If even an ounce of it is true, I have to go to summer school.* And the big deal of that was that my father *paid* for it. I remembered it being really expensive. But my dad cared enough to take care of it. All I can remember about that summer was that it was so *hot* because the school had no air conditioning. Thanks to my father, who forced me to straighten out that summer, things did turn around. I passed all the summer school classes and accumulated enough credits to return to school. So, when sophomore year started, I was doing better. I was focused and I felt more comfortable. At this point, I was back to getting A's and B's. I was moving forward again.

*   *   *   *   *

Later that year, another momentous *move* occurred when my mom and I left LeFrak City for an apartment in Flushing, Queens.

47

Crime was high in the neighborhood and it felt unsafe. Drugs were rampant. Wherever you went in LeFrak, you smelled pot. A number of my sister's friends had died from heroin overdoses in the late sixties and early seventies. I think that scared my mother.

It was now just me and Mom living together. We were renting out the ground floor of a small two-bedroom apartment that was owned by an Indian family. They were very nice people but didn't believe in killing cockroaches because it violated their religious beliefs. As a result, we had roaches crawling all over the place. Cherie came over to check things out. As we were about to start unpacking our boxes, she stopped us. First, she went to the grocery store and bought all kinds of cockroach killers. And then, gross as it was, she was literally scooping up the roaches (hundreds) up with a dustpan and throwing them out. Cherie was great like that—very practical. She then sprayed down the entire apartment. By the time she left, the roach situation was under control. She was the adult in the room who was able to help me and Mom move onward.

During this period, Mom was still working, hopping from job to job when she could function. I would lose track. Is she working for Kelly Services or for the CEO of Philip Morris or for Diane von Furstenberg? I was never sure. She would sometimes get a job for just a few weeks at Kelly Services. They would tell her, "We only need an executive secretary for three weeks." And the next thing you know, she was there for an extended period of time, like four months. This was because they liked her work and wanted to keep her. And even when she was still drinking, she often managed to function. But sooner or later she would go on a bender and then she would stop going to work.

But I was used to Mom's behavior and basically ignored it. I was mostly focused on exploring my new neighborhood and making friends in school.

One day, on the way to school, at the bus stop on 149th Street and Northern Boulevard, I met a guy named Bob Bellusci, who wound up becoming my best friend, a tremendously positive influence on my life.

Bob was a quiet, unassuming guy. But his laid-back demeanor was deceiving because he was an intensely competitive super-athlete. When it came to swimming, he was the fastest free-styler in our high school. He was also the captain of the basket-ball team. (He and I were the only white guys playing on the high school team, and some guys joked that I only got on the team to keep Bob company.) As for baseball, he was a fantastic pitcher and wound up pitching in the city championships at Yankee Stadium. And during the playoffs he beat the famed John Franco, who went on to have a great career with the New York Mets. He was terrific. (He's still a great athlete today. At age sixty-four, he's a black belt in two forms of martial arts, and from the neck down, his body looks like a thirty-year-old.)

When we met outside at the bus stop, we quickly realized we were in the same classes, so he talked me into joining the swimming team. I was the *second-best* backstroker in school. A guy named Michael P. was the best. He could have been another Mark Spitz. But he stopped showing up at practice, which was good for me. Without Michael around, number two was moving up toward the top slot. I liked that recognition. And I liked being part of a team. Bob and I would go to practices together. And we would be on the bus together.

After school, because Bob had three brothers and a sister, we would try to get rides home from his older brothers. And with Bob as a steady influence, I was much more disciplined than I had ever been. I was no longer cutting class or skipping practice. I was also going to school every day, doing much better with less unstructured time. And since we had moved away from LeFrak, I wasn't hanging out in that barbershop anymore either.

Instead, I was literally using my hair to get ahead. When I was fifteen or sixteen, my sister Cherie had a friend who recommended me for a modeling job in the men's hair-cutting industry. I learned that there are world-renowned competitions, serious contests for hair cutting and hair modeling. These hair cutters are superstars in their industry. And Cherie's friend recommended that I try out as a hair model at the New York State Convention Center. I remember being thrust into this whole world that I had no idea existed—hair-cutting contests for men that were global events.

On the first day I went, they cut my hair and paid me $35! That's $187 in today's money, which was a big deal to me as a sixteen-year-old. After my hair was finished, I then became part of the show, an exhibition assessed by the judges who were ruling on the best haircut of the day. That started my part-time work as a hair model. I loved it.

Whenever I would do these competitions, we always placed very high. One day at the competition one of the hair cutters named Sal Fodera came up to me and said, "You have great hair. Can I give you my card?" I never did call him. But then, months later, he recognized me coming out of the F train by 179th Street, right near the Midland Bar.

"You never called me," he exclaimed, smiling. "I was very serious. You will make money."

This time around I did call and found out that Sal had a famous hair salon at the Warwick Hotel and cut *everybody's* hair—superstars and celebrities, including athletes like hockey star Ron Dugay, business magnates like Potamkin from the Cadillac company, and even movie stars too, like Cary Grant. As Sal would tell me, Potamkin would come in for a little snippet, a comb out almost every day. Anyway, this guy was famous himself, and he wound up using *me* to train his other hair cutters on how to cut hair. There I was, at age sixteen, getting paid $50 to have my hair cut. I was a guinea pig. But they called it a "modeling" job. After all these haircuts, my hair would be very short. And my friends goofed on me because my hair was so short.

I also participated in the haircutting competitions with Sal's brother Vinny, who was also a great haircutter. I loved Vinny. He once gave me a phenomenal haircut at a contest in New Jersey. I was learning and listening to world-class hair cutters, observing the judges, and watching all the action. Vinny won the trophy that day. Forty years later, he walked into my office and handed me the trophy and said, "It's your turn to have this," and I still do. I knew what a good haircut was! This was a whole new world unto itself.[1] I moved into this whole new space and embraced it.

Between going to school, hanging out with my high school friends, and modeling, I was living more of a normal life. Mom was still drinking and in bad shape, and Dad was basically MIA. But I was an independent, driven seventeen-year-old, excited about my high school friends, athletics, and girls. A rough home life was not going to stop me. I was moving forward.

---

1 Vinny, who is now eighty-two, still cuts my hair! And he wound up cutting my son's hair too, which is a delicate thing to do. It's difficult for some autistic people to tolerate a haircut, but Vinny had incredible control over my son. It's a gift.

CHAPTER 3

The Drinking Man

He says, "Bill, I believe this is killing me"
As a smile ran away from his face
"Well, I'm sure that I could be a movie star
If I could get out of this place"

—"Piano Man," Billy Joel (1973)

━━━━━━━━━━ ♫ ━━━━━━━━━━

The date was February 4, 1977. It was my seventeenth birthday. And I was in a great mood.

That afternoon after classes and basketball practice, I was heading home from John Bowne High School when my buddy Bob Bellusci saw me waking down the steps. He waved me over and guided me straight toward a group of his friends who I'd never met before. These introductions would change my life forever.

Bob's inner circle consisted of three seventeen-year-old girls—Amy Rice, Anita Rothberg, and Taryn Soba—and two guys, Richie Chin and Walter Silva. Everybody seemed incredibly friendly, outgoing, and intelligent. From the moment I met them, I could see that they were fantastic people. I don't know how we had never met before, but it was all happening on my birthday.

All three girls were very pretty. Anita was the most attractive of the three, with perfect facial features, with beautiful eyes and a great smile. All of them were a bit nerdy, with their thick eyeglasses and conservative clothing. As I would discover, Amy, Anita, and Taryn were all good students with top grades and conscientious about their schoolwork. Amy was a particularly excellent student, a goody-two-shoes type when it came to pleasing the teachers and doing everything perfectly. Anita was very funny and would blurt things out that would make everyone laugh, especially herself. She loved her own jokes. Taryn, being Dominican, had this wonderful caramel-colored skin, and she had great social skills and was a great conversationalist.

As for Bob's buddies, Richie was a very good-looking guy, who was also a great student, though not particularly athletic. (As I mentioned earlier, it was Bob who was the super-athlete, a top competitor on the swimming and basketball teams.) Walter wasn't very athletic either, though he was amazingly smart and charismatic, and he loved music almost as much as me. And unsuspectingly, Walter was also a very sensitive person who always allowed himself to be vulnerable. This quality made him a very attractive human being. Walter also had a great sense of humor—or at least he laughed at my jokes. He would later earn a doctorate in applied mathematics and work for NASA.

We all just clicked, becoming close friends almost over-night. It was as if we had automatically developed a kinship based on personality chemistry and a mutual need for connection. We soon referred to ourselves as The Group, kindred spirits who looked out for each other. Admittedly, we were a little cliquish, but in a good way.

Richie, Amy, and Walter became role models for me because they were so academically minded and disciplined, which made me more conscientious about studying too. As high school seniors, they were all thinking about their futures—what college they would attend, what they would major in, and what they would eventually do professionally. As for me, I wasn't thinking about that stuff at all. I was more into making money at the bar on weekends and hanging out late at night. There was nobody at home saying, "Are you going to college? Where are you going to go?" No such conversation in my house. Both my parents were still drinking heavily and out late at night, anxious to escape their own realities.

My mom and I were still living in Flushing while Dad had a two-bedroom apartment in Jamaica, Queens. Dad was still working at the Midland while Mom was a regular customer up in Flushing at the Murray Hill Pub. In fact, months after I met The Group, Mom got me a job working at the Murray Hill, serving drinks, which was illegal since I wasn't even eighteen yet. But nobody cared. And soon after I started working at Mom's bar, my father got me a job working at the Midland—bartending. I felt like I had arrived in my dad's domain. I'd been going in that bar since I was a little kid, so everybody knew me then as *John's son*. People couldn't technically call me Junior, because my dad and I had different middle names. His was George and mine is Brian. For a period of my life, people starting calling me Brian to differentiate us. This only added to the challenges of discovering my identity and becoming my own person.

In any case, I was really leading a double life—a high school student by day, a bartender by night. While others in high school might be participating in chess or debate clubs, or practicing hoops, working at bars was *my* extracurricular work! I was happily earning money. And to put it bluntly, I was drinking my ass off.

What gave my life some stability at the end of high school was The Group. They all seemed to genuinely care about what I was thinking and doing, and they became like a second family. They made me more aware of what to look for in the future and how to plan ahead. I didn't fully realize it then, but they were very positive influences, a highly therapeutic counterbalance to my nightlife at the bar and to the chaos at home. What glued us together was that we could be vulnerable with one another, sharing secrets and creating an openness that built a sense of trust.

We talked about everything—about our personal lives, dating, school politics, and, of course, our trials and tribulations at home. I shared with them some of the challenges I had growing up with both parents' drinking, a situation that had created an emotional and financial sense of independence in me. In turn, they shared with me issues like their parents' gambling and drug addictions, infidelities, and financial strife.

Aside from the serious exchange of confidences with The Group, there was also a lot of fun and laughter. We had a blast. We all loved music and talked about it constantly. The Group shared my passion for singing and they liked talking about the current music scene. It was the seventies, a wild time, the era of *Saturday Night Fever* (1977), Studio 54, and the disco craze. As high school kids, we were consumed with the idea of going out dancing on weekends. And we would dance and dance and dance.

We became Disco Heads: Every Friday we'd plan out which club we were going to. Were we going to drive into Manhattan and try to get into Studio 54, the Copa, or the exclusive Régine's?[1] Or did we want to be hanging out at our local clubs in Long Island, like the Rusty Nail or Elephas?[2] No matter where we went, we couldn't wait to escape into the world of the dark disco, the throbbing beat of the music, and our favorite singing stars like Gloria Gaynor, the Bee Gees, Diana Ross, the Village People, and Donna Summer. There was nonstop action on the dance floor, which was illuminated by multicolored lasers. No place exemplified the era more than Studio 54. Though it was open for only three years—from April 26, 1977, to February 2, 1980—Studio 54 was arguably the most iconic nightclub to emerge in the twentieth century. Set in a former opera house in midtown Manhattan,

---

1 Régine Zylberberg built a $500 million empire of twenty-three clubs worldwide, the flagship located in the Delmonico Hotel.

2 Elephas was a discotheque on Northern Blvd. at 211th St., Bayside, Queens. It was infamous for being the place where the Son of Sam (David Berkowitz) wounded two people who were sitting in their car outside the club.

with the stage innovatively reenvisioned as a dance floor, Studio 54 became a space of sexual, gender, and creative liberation, where every patron could feel like a star. You never knew who you might see—Calvin Klein, Liza Minnelli, Mick and Bianca Jagger, Richard Gere, Mikhail Baryshnikov, Halston, Grace Jones, or Andy Warhol. One night when I was at Studio 54 before the club got too crowded, I noticed a beautiful woman with her back to the bar, wearing a black-sequined outfit, with her long hair hanging straight back. As the light from the bar illuminated her face, I called her name: "Cheryl?!" She pulled her head up and flashed me that cover girl smile. I just melted. It was Cheryl Tiegs. She was one of the most beautiful women I had ever seen.

Even though we were clubbing every weekend, most of us were not yet of drinking age, though getting into the club was usually no problem. We could maneuver our way in. In my senior year of high school, I turned eighteen, the oldest of my friends by a few months. I was 6'2" and 185 pounds, the most mature looking of The Group, so I just pulled my friends in with me. Also, back then, they didn't check IDs that carefully. It was all about looks. Steve Rubell, the co-owner of Studio 54, pretty much invented the concept of the velvet rope, instigating a ruthlessly capricious nightclub door policy. He either liked your clothes and your looks or he didn't. As high school kids, we wanted to go there and test our luck. But first we had to drive in and find parking. No matter where we went clubbing, I was always the driver because I was the one who got my driver's license first. "I will drive" became my motto.

As high school guys, we were all trying to be cool, like John Travolta, in his leisure suit jackets and tight polyester pants. We learned how to dance to "The Hustle" by Van McCoy and numerous others that were the rage of the era. It was a great time to be alive.

At this time, I was dating a Jewish girl named Toby Abramson. It was the first time I had been with anyone since Laura. It lasted about a year. I had been introduced to Toby by her good friend Amy. In fact, as I learned later, Toby wanted to date me and specifically sought Amy out to connect us. Toby came from a middle-class family. Her father, who was a high school teacher, instilled in Toby and her younger sister a love of learning. (Toby would wind up earning a doctorate in psychology.) Toby was not only super smart and studious but also very pretty, with beautiful green eyes and a great figure. She had it all and would become our senior class president.

Even though I was dating Toby, more and more I was becoming close to Amy, who was equally attractive. Not only was she beautiful with bright brown doe-like eyes but she had a warmth and confidence about her that was unusual for her age. Although she was maybe only five feet tall, she had an imposing presence about her, an understanding of life and money and the way the world worked. So even though she was sweet and inno-cent, she was also very shrewd and insightful. I would call her a free spirit and a quick learner. She was quietly more worldly than most of her peers.

I really liked her, and we became confidantes. We just

seemed to connect and always had a meeting of the minds. We would talk on the phone for hours. (In fact, we even had a song we liked called "Telephone Line" by the Electric Light Orchestra.) In some ways, we were very similar. Both of us had independent personalities. And both of us had higher aspirations. Our fathers had both been entrepreneurs. Her dad was a CPA and had his own business. Although he did well, the family wasn't "rich" by any definition. But compared to most of us in The Group, it felt like Amy was better off, a bit more comfortable, though not rich. She just wasn't struggling.

I think we instinctively knew that Amy and I could, one day, create our own prosperous lives by watching what our fathers had done. I felt as if her father's spirit had been passed down to her. And that made us unwittingly compatible at the age of eighteen. We didn't know that at the time, but I think we knew that it was up to us to create what we wanted to do or to be.

When it came to interplay with Amy, I was a flirt and an entertainer. Whenever I saw her in the hallways, to gain her attention, I would break out into my rendition of "Rich Girl" by Hall and Oates. She was the rich girl, and I would sing to her that it didn't matter anyway, I knew we were going to be together.

She would always laugh at me singing this.

And although I was dating Toby, I was slowly, unbeknownst to me, really falling in love with Amy. It happened slowly. Back then, we would all hang out at a pizza place in Flushing called Angelo's or at the Palace Diner. We stayed up as late as we could and talked about music and sports and whatever was culturally relevant at the time, typical teenage things. Then on weekends, we would all go out to the clubs as much as possible.

One night, when I was eighteen, I remember being in the Copa and dancing with Amy when Barry Manilow's song "Copacabana" started to play. Amy and I were dancing closely. And as cliché as it sounds, the attraction between us was like a magnet. So just as we were dancing, I kissed Amy on her lips. That was our first kiss. And that kiss would be the start of something more meaningful than I would ever imagine.

*   *   *   *   *

All at the same time as my crazy period of bartending, discos, drinking, clubs, and car accidents, I was very much trying to "find myself." One of the creative outlets that I did not want to leave behind was my love of singing. I started taking voice lessons in Manhattan with a renowned vocal coach named Nanci Sorin Collyer. She gave lessons at her Lincoln Center studio. She was very well respected, having worked with many of the biggest names on Broadway. I was committed to taking these lessons. No less than forty times a year, I took the F train from Jamaica, Queens, to Manhattan on a Saturday afternoon, often just hours before I went out partying or bartending for the night. While I was abusing myself with alcohol, I was still channeling some of my energy toward something that was meaningful to me. Of course, singing and drinking don't mix. When it comes to your throat, smokey bars weren't a help either, nor was snorting coke and staying out until 5:00 a.m. Eventually I started having a chronic sore throat and laryngitis. It got to the point where it seemed as if I was taking antibiotics all the time. I continued to take singing lessons through all of this.

This pattern continued until age nineteen, when I finally consulted with a German physician named Dr. Buchbinder, an elderly man who was short in stature and spoke with a very heavy accent. There was something about him that I found endearing. And I think I trusted him because of his age. It was Dr. Buchbinder who recommended that the cure to my throat problems was a tonsillectomy, something that many people do when they're kids. The surgery was scheduled to be performed at Deepdale Hospital (which did not have a great reputation) in Little Neck, Queens. I was all set to do it. But just a few days before the surgery, my health insurance company informed me that I had a high deductible for the anesthesia. Basically, I would have no coverage for it. When I consulted with Dr. Buchbinder, he inadvisably told me that he could do the surgery under local anesthesia if I could not come up with the money. I was naive and anxious, and wanted my health to improve, so after considering it just for a minute, I elected to proceed.

Enter the dark ages: On the day of the procedure, I was led down to the hospital's basement, in the belly of the building, into an archaic, antiquated operating room that looked like it had last been used for surgery decades before. Standing there with Dr. Buchbinder were his two nurses. One of them was a large, muscular woman who was taller than I was. I would later learn that she was there to hold me down. She reminded me of the cartoon comic strip character Brunhilda. She told me what to expect in the next half hour and then administered a drug to relax me, probably Demerol.

Hovering over me was the diminutive Dr. Buchbinder, glasses on and wearing what was then called a head mirror with lights on it to illuminate the patient, something you'd see in an old movie. I found myself wondering what went on first, his glasses or the light.

Next, I was placed in a cheap stacking chair, one with a scratched metal frame and a red, torn vinyl seat. Then I was blind-folded! After that indignity, a clamp was placed in my mouth to hold it wide open. That was uncomfortable, to say the least. Then I was given a few shots of Lidocaine to help numb the pain.

I remember that the three of them conferred in a whisper, and suddenly Dr. Buchbinder moved very close. Though I was blindfolded, I could feel his breath on me. Brunhilda was instructed to stand behind me and "secure the patient," as if this were a torture chamber. She then placed both of her massive hands on my shoulders, pressed me down, and kept me pinned to the red vinyl chair.

Dr. Buchbinder, using a scalpel, entered my throat and began to cut. Because of the proximity of the back of the throat to my eardrum, I could hear the cutting, Grrrrrrrrr. Oh God, the sound of one's own flesh being shredded was awful. Then, even worse, I felt warm blood flooding into my mouth. Though the doctor was trying to suction it out as quickly as he could, it was hard to keep up. There was too much blood in my mouth, not enough suction, and I was coughing (though I was told *not* to, as coughing would only increase the bleeding). Damn, I was trying so hard not to cough. But I felt like I was choking to death. At this point, Dr. Buchbinder was working like a mad scientist, his pace almost frantic. With his face just an inch or two from mine, I could feel him panting over me. This entire scene—from the dusty basement room to the cheap chair, to being blindfolded and then cut while awake—was a scene from a horror movie.

About an hour later, I was lying in recovery only to be awakened by Dr. Buchbinder. He was close to me, but not so close as he had been. "It went well," he said. "You'll be healed in two weeks and then come back for a follow-up." As he walked away, I could not help wondering if he had even noticed the many specs of my blood still on his glasses. So much for hygiene.

Despite the seemingly barbaric conditions, I never regretted the tonsillectomy. The operation was a success, and I subsequently had far fewer throat issues. Dr. Buchbinder is long gone, as is Deepdale, which closed in 1996.

Had I just saved some money and thought more clearly, I might have been able to afford a proper operation with anesthesia. But I was impulsive and wanted it done immediately. It's amazing the insane and unimaginable places our addictions can bring us to.

After I was healed, I continued with my signing lessons. Those lessons were something that I truly enjoyed. Your voice, much like an instrument, is something that you need to learn how to play, and despite all the craziness in other parts of my life, I was learning how to use my own voice.

*   *   *   *   *

As high school ended in June 1978, the close-knit members of The Group were inevitably separated. The emotional ties of high school friends can never be equaled again in life, and it made me sad to leave them all. We would remain lifelong friends. The members of The Group were my role models. They talked about moving on to college, a thought that I never independently had. We supported and were honest with one another. Despite this, the day would come when we would have to go our separate ways.

When it came to college, my parents could not afford a private university, and I was drinking and snorting away all the money I was making in tips at the bar. So, I went to the affordable State University of New York at Stony Brook on a special scholarship from the EOC (Educational Opportunity Centers). This opportunity came to me because of my essay for admission. My language skills allowed me to be exempt from English 101.

While I went to Stony Brook, Amy got into the State University at Albany, which was about a hundred miles away. Over the next few years, I would go up there and spend time with her whenever I could. But during the first few years of college, it was understood that we could see other people. Ours was a distant, teenage puppy love.

Even though I had decided to make the move from high school to college, I wasn't honestly interested in academics or a degree. In some ways, I was less of a kid and more of an adult than the typical college freshman. I had been working for years, making money, going out to clubs, and drinking as much as I could.

As for my college experience, you might say that I kind of *pretended* to go to college at Stony Brook. I went through the motions of going to classes (when I wasn't hungover or sleeping) with a major in English. But my heart wasn't in it. Out of any class I took in college, it was Economics 101 that I enjoyed the most. There were certain principles in that course that I'll remember forever, especially the concept of *opportunity cost*—the money or benefits *lost* by not selecting a particular option during the decision-making process. An opportunity cost is composed of a business's explicit and implicit costs. The idea of it helps businesses understand how one decision over another may affect profitability. Later in life, I came to understand that when you do one thing, it is inevitably costing you the opportunity to do something else. You make a decision, go with it, and don't look back. Sometimes you don't know what the right decision is until after you've made it. However, the paralysis of not making a decision is the worst decision of all. And you stand still. (Aside from economics, I liked all the English classes, including ebonics, urban language, and Black English. That becomes relevant later because, believe it or not, I went on to write hip-hop music.)

Of course, in real life, my youthful decisions back then (blowing off classes and drinking) were definitely costing me *opportunities* that I might otherwise have gained. But when you're young and think you're invincible (and have no guidance), you just do what you want to do. Not surprisingly, I lasted only three semesters in college. I loved partying more. To me, that's where life was really happening. I liked everything about the night-life—the adult conversation, the pulsing music, the drinking, and the drugs.

During freshman year I moved onto a hallway of the dorm with juniors and seniors. And all I did was drink. Although my dormmates were older, they were not necessarily as experienced as me. They told me that they were going to teach *me* how to drink. I found that comical. It was me, as a freshman, who taught *them*. Honestly, I could drink them all under the table. In fact, I would mock them and drink twice as much as they did. They couldn't get over it. It gave me some kind of stupid respect.

In February 1979, on a wild drunken night celebrating my nineteenth birthday, I did something I'd never done before: I took a Quaalude. Bizarrely, that pill had the exact opposite desired effect. Instead of me feeling a sense of euphoria and drowsiness, it made me violent. It was one of the only times I'd ever become physically aggressive. When I was thirteen, I took some martial arts classes. I never forgot what I learned, and on the night of my nineteenth birthday it all came back to me.

That night, in an altered state, I went on a rampage and wound up kicking in a ceramic water fountain in the hallway of the dorm. I literally destroyed it with karate kicks, the entire thing smashed to the floor. I also cracked open a glass showcase with my fist, punching my hand right into the glass. I had shards of glass embedded in my knuckles. For a long time after that, little slivers of glass popped out of my skin, which doctors had told me would happen. That night of violence not only caused me physical pain but also got me into a lot of trouble at school. And I had to do some fast thinking to get out of it.

I charmed the RA (resident assistant), who was a nice woman named Nadine. I knew that she liked me. Standing before her desk, I remember keeping both hands behind my back to hide my right hand, which was heavily bandaged with rings of gauze on it. She looked at me and said, "*Somebody* punched in the glass showcase last night. Would you happen to know *who* did it?"

I brought my right arm from behind my back and scratched my nose with my heavily bandaged hand. And very coyly I said, "I have no idea who did it, but whoever it was, I'm sure *they* feel very bad about it and would apologize." In my own way, I was owning it, but not really. It was a dance between us. She looked at me and said, "I'm sure this person realizes that he could be expelled over this."

"I'm sure the person does," I answered. "And I'm sure he really regrets his actions." She let me go and I walked out. This wasn't the first or the last time that I had managed to talk my way out of a tight situation. I did it all my life. And I went right back to my drinking.

There seemed to be more bars on campus than any college on the East Coast. One semester it was announced that there was going to be a campus-wide beer-drinking contest, the winner getting a bicycle. The contest went on for several weeks with everybody vying for the prize as the students got drunker and drunker on beer. The final contestants came down to me and a "big" girl on campus who was wearing overalls. I remember that she was very sweet, and she almost killed me with her ability to down the beer. By the time she chugged it all down, she had the foam running down the side of the glass while I was still drinking. I couldn't keep up with her. She destroyed me. It was ironic because I had taken singing lessons as a teenager and had great throat control and had always been number one when it came to pouring alcohol straight down my throat, faster than anyone. I had proved that on the staircase in LeFrak City. Yet this girl beat me easily. No longer was I number one when it came to the quick consumption of beer.

Once she had won, I looked at her and said, "How did you *do* that?"

"I have a secret," she answered. "I sing professionally, and I've taken lessons for years. I've learned how to open my throat to allow the beer to go right down." Astonished, I replied, "That's *my* secret. You're just better at it than me!" There you have it, the secret to guzzling beer is singing lessons. Crazy stuff, huh?

At age nineteen, as my academic career was collapsing, my alcohol and drug use was taking over. On weekends and during summers, I was back in Queens, bartending full-time and drinking as much as possible. I had moved from the dorm to living with Dad because I wanted to hang out and drink with him. It was an opportunity to be closer to my father. Ironically, Mom's drinking was unmanageable, and I wanted to escape that environment and her new boyfriend. It felt cooler to live with Dad anyway, and I had more access to a car.

By the time that I was in my late teens, I thought working at the bar was great: All I did was drink and make money. I didn't have to deal with "reality." Amy sometimes talked to me about my drinking. Generally, other than an occasional question from one of my sisters, she was the only one who would come right out and say, "You're drinking too much." All I heard when she did this was "blah, blah, blah." But she didn't overdo it. Instead, she was trying to let me sort it out for myself. When I asked her years later why she didn't push harder, she told me, "I knew you were smart and capable. And I knew you were going to snap out of it. That wasn't you." I don't know how she knew that, because I didn't know it then and it took me years to snap out of it. And despite the late nights and heavy drinking, I still managed to "present well" physically, which hid the severity of my addictions. I dressed well and my hair was always neat.

Amy stuck with me while I was drinking in college. Her dad had got her a car, so she was able to sneak down to Stony Brook and stay with me for the weekend, either in my dorm or at my father's house in Jamaica. We stayed together and her parents never knew. At the time, Amy was the only positive influence in my life.

I was stuck. No ability to move in any direction. I was stuck in the bars, and drinking stopped me from doing *everything* else in life. Drinking stunts your growth and inhibits your movement. You don't progress in any way. You don't make new friends. You don't exercise. You don't eat right. You don't clean your apartment. You stay stuck. You're always either chasing a high or coming down from one. Most mornings, I was completely hungover and would wake up with the TV on, in the middle of the soaps, like *All My Children* with Susan Lucci or *One Life to Live* with Erika Slezak. I was strung out and completely unmotivated. I wasn't interested in sports or singing or hanging out with my old friends, or even reading a book, much less getting a college degree.

In 1980, after three semesters at Stony Brook, I left and transferred to Queens College. Once again, I was kind of pretending to go to school while bartending and snorting coke. I didn't go to class and lasted only a semester. I had registered for classes just to be able to say I was in college. It was ridiculous. My addiction had taken over, and my compulsion to work and make money was empowering. I was working in dive bars six or seven days a week, drinking all the way. And I made a fortune. It was 1979 and I was coming home with a thousand dollars a week in cash. (That was a lot of money, equivalent to four thousand in today's dollars.) I was sure that I could make that kind of money for the rest of my life.

Maybe the desperation I felt for security as a kid instilled in me the craving to make money. In my twenties, I always made more than any of my friends. But I always blew it all—drank and snorted it away.

My father knew what I was doing wasn't healthy. He would refer to the money I was making as *the golden handcuffs*. "You're never going to do anything else," he warned me, knowing how seductive the money could be. "You're never going to progress in life." He was genuinely afraid of that for me. How ironic. My sister Denise said the same thing.

By the time I was twenty-one, my lifestyle was already taking quite a toll on me physically. I started having a lot of stomach pain. It was pretty severe. And I didn't have any health insurance. I mentioned this to Denise, and she somehow arranged for me to see a really good GI doctor on the Upper East Side of Manhattan. To this day, I don't know how she paid for it. It must have been out of her own pocket, and it must have cost a lot of money.

That day, I remember putting on a medical robe and the nurse handing me a malted liquid to drink. They then laid me down on the table and proceeded to give me a complete GI series X-ray, which examines your digestive system. Right afterward, as I got off the table, the nurse directed me down a long hallway toward the doctor's office. I remember grabbing the robe, which was open behind me, clutching it closed. As I walked down the hall and stood in the doorway, there were two doctors conferring with their backs to me, looking up at an X-ray on a light box. I cleared my throat so they would know I was standing there. As they turned around and look at me, they seemed perplexed. "Can we help you?"

"Yes, my name's John Beyer."

They looked astonished. With wide eyes, one of the doctors exclaimed, "*You're* John Beyer? Based on your X-ray, we were expecting somebody eighty years old! What are you doing to your stomach?" Of course, it was the alcohol. At twenty-one, I had already done a lot of physical damage to myself. And I remember being asked by the doctor about my diet and lying to him about how much I was actually drinking. I had the distinct feeling that he could see right through me. And I left there with a prescription, which relieved a lot of the pain in my stomach, though I continued to drink anyway.

Shortly after that, in the summer of 1981, Denise dragged me to a therapist. She knew I was depressed. And, of course, she had a sense of how much I was drinking. But she never really lectured me about it. She was maternal, looking after me like she always did because she knew I was in trouble.

The therapist, Dr. Ron Hanover, a PhD psychologist, was associated with the local VA hospital, the same one where my father would be hospitalized later that year. Ron was a specialist in PTSD and addiction for veterans. And while I wasn't a veteran, I qualified to be a patient. I started seeing Ron at age twenty-one and continued seeing him for decades, forty or fifty times a year. We communicate to this day.

I talked to him about the pain and the emptiness I felt, about my growing up years in LeFrak, about my parents' drinking, about work, and about my relationship with Amy. And of course, I would talk about my struggle with drinking. But he never pushed AA on me. That had to happen when I was ready. And I wasn't ready then.

When I was behind the bar, I felt invincible. I served drinks like a machine. I was good at it. I was a performer. I would often sing along with the jukebox, and I sometimes danced behind the bar as well. I was popular. I had a following. I liked how that made me feel. People would come into the bar and ask for me. They knew my name. This gave me the attention that I craved. I got everybody all revved up, crazy. I'd get some of the girls to get up on top of the bar, doing high kicks like the Rockettes. Crazy stuff like that became everyday events. It was an adrenaline high that gave me a kind of notoriety, a little cachet. And I thought it would never stop. I did not want it to stop.

Even though I was having such success in the bars, I knew underneath that it was bad for me. It was a voice in the back of my head that said the job was just feeding the alcoholism and the coke abuse.

Was there a lot of coke? Yes. It all started with my first line of cocaine, which I took with two casual friends from the Murray Hill bar—my drinking buddies, Victor and Maureen. Both would turn out to be lifelong friends.

One night at Kissena Park, a 235-acre park in Flushing, I snorted my first line of cocaine off the top of a boombox. I abused cocaine only because it enabled me to drink more. And I very rarely drank or snorted in the morning, except years later when I was bottoming out. Although I would not consider myself a coke *addict*, it's obviously highly addictive and creates a craving for even more coke. And it wasn't just me snorting. I was a liaison. A customer would come into the bar and say they wanted to "cop some coke" and I would hook them up with a dealer. He, in turn, would give me some free coke. Both the customer and the dealer would thank me! Everybody left happy.

In my early twenties, when closing up the Midland one night, I was leaving with my dealer, Carlos. Carlos always wore a couple of heavy wristbands, always on the same wrist, though I never knew why. One day after I pressed him about it, he showed me what was under the wristbands. The underside of his left wrist looked like it was carved out. He was missing half of it. In a drug deal that had gone bad, he had taken a bullet that obliterated most of his wrist. He was lucky he still had his hand attached to his arm. Though he was a drug dealer, Carlos was a pretty decent guy. He just wanted to make money. And selling coke was how he knew how to do it.

That night as I left the bar with Carlos, I said, "I need more coke." He didn't have any. "But come with me, Brian," as he used to call me. He took me to an abandoned house in South Jamaica, Queens, that had become a shooting gallery—everybody there was getting high on *something*. Some were smoking pot, others were freebasing or smoking cocaine, and some were shooting heroin. There were about a dozen people in various corners huddled in the shadows, in little groups. I was the only white guy there, but I felt totally comfortable.

As I walked in, everybody looked up, their eyes darting around. You could tell they were all assessing what drug I might be looking for. I had been in a shooting gallery only one time before. Anyway, Carlos went into a dark corner, and he emerged with the coke we came for. I was observing somebody shoot heroin. The guy was about eight feet away from me with the proverbial rubber strap around his upper arm. The needle was going in. And he had such a look of relaxed euphoria, ecstasy on his face. I immediately wanted to try it. I yearned for it.

75

I said, "Carlos, hook me up. I want to do that." I was really curious about the high I would get. But he looked at me, shook his head, and refused. "No, Brian, not you. You're not gonna do that." To this day, I have never tried heroin. I have no idea where Carlos is or what happened to him, but I'm very grateful for how he protected me that night. It just shows you how being an addict can escalate and can trap you. I came so very close to heroin use. But Carlos saved me.

Alcohol was clearly taking me to places I had never been. It was a downward spiral. You drink and drink and drink, and you do the coke to drink even more. And then all of a sudden you find yourself in a shooting gallery and heroin looks good to you. You lose your rational thinking. This is a far cry from the little boy who was brought in front of the eighth graders as an example of what to look and act like.

Being in that shooting gallery reminds me of the lyrics from the song "Everybody Plays the Fool" by The Main Ingredient. "How can you help it when the music starts to play and your ability to reason is swept away?" My reasoning was completely distorted by alcohol.

*　　*　　*　　*　　*

When I was twenty and working at the Murray Hill Pub, a fellow bartender, Jimmy Fox, became a good friend of mine. He was a very good-looking guy and a very caring person. He had a great personality. He was warm, and people loved him.

At times, we backed each other up behind the bar. If I had to take a break to snort a line, he would jump in behind the bar for ten minutes and vice versa. We both partied all the time and did crazy things. Like at 3:00 a.m., we'd take a bet: Who could do twenty-five push-ups faster on the yellow lines of Northern Boulevard? The winner would get the extra line of coke. This was insane alcohol-and-drug-induced behavior. But we couldn't get enough of it.

As I got to know Jimmy better, I could see that despite his many positive personal attributes, he was severely depressed. One thing that frustrated him was that he could talk to women, but he felt like he could never close the deal. He felt *less than*. Maybe it was because he was a little overweight. I don't know.

Although Jimmy was always in the bar, one night he was conspicuously absent. I called his house and his brother Freddy said he wasn't sure where Jimmy was. The family had been away. "Jimmy didn't go with us. I'll go upstairs to see if he's there."

At the same time, I was both holding the phone to my ear and pouring drinks. I heard some commotion going on in the background. Freddy came back to the phone and abruptly said, "Jimmy's not here. I gotta go, I'll call you later." And he hung up. I thought to myself, *This a little odd. Where the hell is Jimmy? He's always here at the bar.* And just minutes later, Lorraine, one of the regular customers, walked in and said, "Yeah, I just passed Jimmy Fox's house, all kinds of cops and ambulances are out front."

I knew something was very wrong. I put somebody behind the bar and I raced down to Jimmy's house. When I got there, I pulled one of the cops to the side and I said, "Is he alive?" And the cop just shook his head no. They found pieces of Jimmy's skull in the schoolyard across the street. He had taken a shotgun, put it in his mouth, and blew off the top of his head.

I was hysterical. I couldn't go back to the bar. I couldn't function. I went down the block to another bar, to a pay phone, and called my dad as tears were streaming down my face.

"Jimmy's dead. Jimmy's dead," I cried into the phone. And I then explained what happened. My father, who could be very philosophical and calm, took in what I said.

"Son, I'm sorry, but just remember: Life is for the living. Life will go on. Life is for the living." And he repeated that phrase again and again. "Life is for the living . . . life will go on."

CHAPTER 4

SCARS

Hello darkness, my old friend
I've come to talk with you again

—"THE SOUND OF SILENCE," SIMON & GARFUNKEL (1964)

AFTER JIMMY'S DEATH, I was inconsolable and continued to drink. I was filled with self-pity. It was *poor me, poor me, POUR me a drink.* If anything, Jimmy's death prompted me to drink even more in an attempt to numb my grief.

I was around twenty and working at the Murray Hill Pub in Flushing, while living in Jamaica with Dad. I was driving my dad's '72 Cutlass Supreme, which was in pretty good shape. Dad had just put a lot of money into getting the car serviced, with new breaks in the front end, ball joints, and tie-rods. It was a nice, fast car, and Dad let me take it out all the time. I would drive to and from work, often driving drunk.

One weekend in July I worked a Friday night at Murray Hill, did a lot of coke, stayed up all night, and then went to an after-hours club. The binge continued the next morning with day drinking at the Midland Bar. Later that day, I went back to work at the Murray Hill at 6:00 p.m. I was coasting on adrenaline and coke. I was so bleary-eyed that I was having trouble talking intelligently. That night at the bar, which had been very busy, I left with a pocket full of money. Then I went back to the after-hours club where I got more coke. I stayed there until 8:00 a.m. By this point, I had been up for forty-eight hours without any sleep! I was really out of my mind.

I was drunk behind the wheel, driving from Flushing to Jamaica, though obviously in no shape to do it. As I was heading south on Utopia Parkway, just before I got to Union Turnpike by St. John's University, I passed out. I just fell asleep behind the wheel! From the police reports, I later learned that I had gone through a red light at 40 mph and broadsided a car with two passengers in it, an elderly couple.

While the driving husband had only a minor scratch on his forehead, the crash did a lot of damage to his wife. Her pelvic bone was broken in multiple places. And the fire department had to use the jaws of life to get her out, as the entire car was demolished. She was in pretty bad shape.

As for me, the impact of the crash had caused me to slam my chin into the hard plastic steering wheel, which was unpadded, unlike today. Back then, there were seatbelts but no shoulder straps to brace for the impact. So, when I hit the wheel, the impact opened up a deep gash along my jawline. (I would wind up with a three-inch scar because of it.)

I was drunk and in shock at the time, and I had to kick the door open to escape from the car. As I staggered out, the husband, the driver of the other car, actually helped *me* because he saw me bleeding so profusely. The blood was everywhere, dripping down all over my clothes and saturating my jeans right through to my underwear. Before the man's wife was taken away in the ambulance, the husband helped me into a different ambulance. And because there was no room in his wife's ambulance, we rode together to the hospital.

Once I got to the emergency room, the ER doctors X-rayed my jaw to see if it was broken, which it wasn't. But the wound was very deep, right down to the bone. I needed forty stitches: twenty on the inside near the bone and twenty near the surface, right across my chin and jawline. At this point, they had contacted my dad to come to the hospital. But on a Sunday morning at 11:00 a.m., Dad was completely hungover. He arrived at the hospital disheveled and smelling of alcohol. When he walked in to see me, the doctor took one look at him and said under his breath, "Boy, the apple doesn't fall far from the tree." He could tell that we were both drunks.

Due to my negligence, I wound up being sued by the couple for $2.9 million! But I had only $40,000 of liability insurance on the car. I was a nineteen-year-old who was essentially broke, so what were they going to take? I was fortunate to have a pretty good attorney appointed to me by my insurance company. When we first met, he asked me what I did for a living. There I was, a bartender who was often drunk with red eyes and strung out on cocaine. I was pretty red in the face and felt leery of telling him about my lifestyle. So, I came up with a more appealing version of myself: I told him that I had been trying to do some modeling and voiceover work and that I had had some headshots recently taken. His eyes darted up when he heard this. "Get me the headshots," he told me. I couldn't imagine why he wanted them.

The case went on for the next three years, with dozens of witness statements and examinations uncovering all kinds of evidence, like the tread marks of the cars, the breaking distance, the color of the traffic light at impact, you name it. It was a mess. There were multiple affidavits asking me about whether I had lost control of the car or had fallen asleep at the wheel. The case went to trial in 1983. I am not proud of my conduct. I am very sorry for what occurred that day. There were dozens of contradictory witness statements testifying that they had been at the intersection on their way to church and saw me go through the red light. It was 9:00 a.m., so there was plenty of light and no doubt about it.

During the very same time, to add to the trauma of it all, Dad's health was failing as he continued to drink. As a result of his previous heart attacks, he had a damaged heart that required regular visits to his cardiologist, Dr. Flateau. I was in the room with Dad one day when the doctor bluntly told him, "John, if you don't stop drinking, you're going to die." And my father said, "I know."

It was ironic that I was supporting Dad's abstinence while I was still in full drinking mode. Dad decided to stop. He took his last drink on New Year's Eve, December 31, 1978. He didn't drink for all of 1979. It was amazing. He knew that he had done so much harm to his body, and he was really trying to turn it around.

But he still showed up at the bar every night, sipping a Coca-Cola. He would bring his books and sit at the bar reading novels underneath the soffit of the bar as the music from the jukebox blared, with people all around him talking loudly. Yet he could concentrate. While he was sober, he had more color in his face, the ashen pallor gone. He not only looked healthier and more vibrant but was also more energetic. It was really very nice to see. He brushed his teeth more regularly and he was no longer wearing the same shirt two days in a row.

At the same time, something strange and beautiful also happened. Mom had a tremendous health scare of her own. While Dad was in this turnaround phase, Mom was drunk almost all the time, on a continual bender, sometimes in a blackout. In the midst of this, she was complaining about a pain in her lower right-hand side. My sisters and I weren't sure if what she said was just an excuse for her to continue drinking, as if to numb the pain. In the past, I often ignored Mom's physical complaints, figuring she wasn't coherent.

But one day she was in so much stomach pain that I took her to the hospital. As it turned out, her white blood count was through the roof, "greater than 10,500 cells," the doctor said, a number that made no sense to me. She was admitted immediately. After multiple tests and no clear diagnosis, the ER doctors did exploratory surgery. They discovered that my mother's appendix had burst, and the gangrene poison had spread throughout her system. It seemed as if she might die. She had remained in critical condition after having major surgery that day, but it saved her life.

When she came out of the hospital, Mom was in really bad shape. For months, she took massive doses of antibiotics and special medicated baths to prevent infection. And as she went through this ordeal, she also detoxed from alcohol. Mom never drank again, not for the rest of her life! She amazingly became a different person—lovely, lively, warm, and outgoing. It was a total transformation, a wonderful thing to see. She was like the old nondrinking Mom—fun, talkative, responsive, and responsible. She even started to steadily work again. Soon, she got a new job in charge of the stenography pool at a major law firm. My mom was sober. And although I was drinking more than ever, I still became very grateful to experience my mom in an entirely new way.

I cannot say the same for Dad. Exactly one year after he put down his drink, on New Year's Eve 1979, he picked up a drink and it all began again. The downward slide was inevitable. Alcoholism is a disease, and the progression of it never goes away. As I would later learn, there is a saying in AA that no matter how long you're sober, the disease is still there, doing proverbial "push-ups" in the parking lot, and relapse is never off the table. So even if you put down the drink, the minute you pick it up again, you're going to start drinking as much as before, if not more. I witnessed this to be 1,000 percent true.

Only ten weeks later, on St. Patrick's Day, March 17, Dad was admitted into the hospital due to liver failure. The disease was winning. By this point his liver was shutting down and he was turning yellow. And his heart was so weak that his legs were ulcerated and swelling, his circulation compromised. He was only fifty-five years old!

Although Dad was so seriously ill in the hospital, Cherie had been planning her wedding and was getting married on June 6. Dad wanted to walk her down the aisle, so after pleading to doctors to let him out for the wedding, he was left in my care on a forty-eight-hour discharge. At the hotel up in Westchester, Dad was moaning in his sleep, in pain from his ulcerated legs. I had trouble sleeping too.

The following day, we all got dressed and the wedding went off without a hitch. When you look at the pictures from that day, Dad looks like he's eighty, not in his fifties. He is ghostly, ashen, and drawn. My sister was actually walking *him* down the aisle, holding him up, not the other way around. Despite his condition, we all put on happy faces. At the wedding I sang the great Andy Williams ballad "More," the song that my mother had asked me to sing over and over again in my childhood. Mom, who was sober at the time, was very proud to be there and hear me.

After the ceremony, Dad went back to the hospital immediately. His condition continued to deteriorate. Shortly after Cherie's wedding, he was transferred to the VA hospital.

As time passed, Dad seemed to kind of shrink as a person in every way. He became very quiet. After all those years of drinking, he was non compos mentis at times.[1] Ironically, that was the term Dad used to use about *other* people in the bar who were very drunk and losing it mentally. And now that's what he had become.

I remember going to visit him in the hospital right toward the very end of his life. I was twenty-one and kind of afraid of what I would see in his room. As the doctor explained, his liver had continued to deteriorate, and it could no longer filter the toxins in his system. I think the poisons had gone to his brain. A few days later I got called to the hospital in the middle of the night by a nurse who told me, "You have to come right away because your father is behaving irrationally."

I remember walking down the dimly lit hall of that hospital toward my dad, who was sitting in a wheelchair. The nurses had taken a cane and stuck it into the spokes of the chair so he couldn't go anywhere. And his wrists were bound to the chair with gauze! It was tragic. He looked up at me as I approached him. "What are you doing here? You're supposed to be dead," he said. He was hallucinating. Here was this brilliant, formerly charismatic man now just a shell of himself. It made me cry.

By this point in their lives, although both my parents had very serious long-term relationships (Mom with a man named Jim, and Dad with a woman named Diane), they still cared for each other a great deal. There was a tenderness between them. So, one day during the terrible year my father was dying, my mom came to visit him in the hospital. And as she saw him, her heart

---

1 As I would later learn, alcohol interferes with the brain's pathways and makes it harder for the brain to control memory, speech, and judgment.

broke. He sat there struggling to stay alive. During the visit, he was able to conjure up enough energy to sit on the edge of his bed as I was standing by the doorway watching. "Gerry," he said, "when I get outta here, let's you and me get married again. We belong together."

As I watched this scene play out, with my father in such vulnerable health, the tears were rolling down my face. I was twenty-one at the time, but I think the little kid inside me always wanted my parents to be back together again.

After that night, I never had much more conversation with Dad. He died weeks later, on September 13, 1981, at fifty-six years old. Although the death certificate stated that he died of heart disease, the real cause of death was acute alcoholism. Dad's brain and organs were destroyed by it. Meanwhile, here I was still on trial for a crime I committed due to my own alcoholism. But the grief of my father's passing didn't stop my drinking at all. It just continued.

After Dad's death I felt lost and angry. In the midst of my grief, there was also family friction. At the time of Dad's death, there was a family fight about who would be the beneficiary of his life insurance policies. Dad wanted the money to be left to my mom and to his three kids. And he verbalized that wish to me and my sisters before he died. Yet somehow the beneficiary forms were changed. When Dad was in the hospital, his then-girlfriend Diane propped him up in bed and had him sign the forms. It was a small policy, just nickels. But the whole series of events led to our family fighting over it. All this just illustrated the insanity of alcoholism and how it can create unmanage-ability in the family.

During this horrible period, the only constant in my life was Amy. The connection between us never wavered. It never, never went away.

* * * * *

Dad was right. Life goes on—as did my trial. Two years after my father died, I was found guilty at age twenty-three. On the warm June morning when the verdict came down, nobody was there for me. Not my sisters. Not my mom. Not even Amy. I was hiding this case as much as I could from all of them. I was so ashamed, so I had to fend for myself. Since I had no money and little insurance, I was now responsible to pay $125,000, though I had only the $40,000 of insurance coverage. What about the balance? One key point that came out during the trial was that the older couple was driving a Hertz *rental* car. My attorney made the most of that and argued to Hertz that there might have been something wrong with the rental car itself. And he urged them to pick up the $85,000 balance so that "this young aspiring model doesn't sue Hertz for future income." They had all my headshots in their hands, me looking perfect, very clean-cut with a great head of hair. Hertz willingly picked up the $85,000 balance if I signed off that I would not sue them. I walked out of the courtroom scot-free. The settlement didn't cost me anything. I learned absolutely nothing. I was immature and irre-sponsible, a full-blown alcoholic. I'm just lucky the woman didn't die. I kept on drinking. After the trial, I went straight to the bar and continued to drink! I had gotten away with it. Perhaps not exactly scot-free. After all, I had scars inside and out.

About a year and a half after the trial ended, something else happened that shattered my world. Late in 1983, Mom started complaining about her back pain and an overall feeling of fatigue. She went to the Mayo Clinic, got a full physical, and everything seemed to check out okay. They told her that she felt poorly because she had emphysema. She had to stop smoking. Although she cut it down, she never stopped. The fatigue and pain persisted. She next consulted with a pulmonologist for further tests. That's when she got the bad news: She had a tiny tumor on her lung, barely discernible on the X-rays. But the really bad news was that the tumor had metastasized, meaning that the cancer cells had broken away from the lung and were forming new tumors in other parts of her body. She was given six months to a year to live.

I felt a blow to my heart. It was surreal. I had dealt with so much death already. This was too much. My sisters and Amy and I watched for months as Mom deteriorated from the advancing cancer and the chemo. There she was, dying a long, slow, horrible death from lung cancer at a time in her life when she had finally stopped drinking. It was tragic watching her lose her hair and resort to wigs. Making matters worse, at this same time Amy's mother got sick too. After being taken by ambulance to the hospital for pain, she was diagnosed with a massive cancerous tumor in her chest cavity. It was inoperable. And she died just a few weeks later.

Outside the synagogue at the funeral, I will never forget the vision of my mom *still* smoking. As she lit up a cigarette, she turned to me and said, "I know I'm next."

Throughout this entire time, despite my own drinking, I somehow met my responsibilities for taking care of Mom, bringing her to chemo and to her doctor appointments. Amy was a gem at the time, helping my family go through mountains of insurance paperwork and hospital bills. In the midst of her own grief, losing her mom, it was so impressive that she was also helping us. Both my sisters and I were incredibly grateful to her.

Mom died just nine months after her diagnosis. The memory of her funeral is a blur. I was almost dazed by it. Within a very short amount of time, both Amy and I had lost our mothers to the same thing—lung cancer. Both had smoked up to four packs of cigarettes a day. At one point, their hospital stays had overlapped, bouncing Amy and me from one hospital room to another.

My mother's story of addiction is a complicated and tragic one, just like Dad's. And Mom suffered a lot because of it. They both did. But I will always be grateful for having that period of two years when my mom stopped drinking. Seeing her completely lucid and in control and loving toward us is how I always want to remember her. Her sobriety was a gift. Yet the pain of experiencing her death just a few years after my dad's death only exacerbated my own drinking. I couldn't stop.

Amy knew, of course, that I was powerless over drinking, but she was helpless in her own way and didn't know what to do with me. As she reflects,

I was young and didn't really understand the impact that drinking had on John or our relationship. I made friends at the bars where he was working, so his bartending became a big part of my social life. I remember being very frustrated and sad when he wasn't working and would stand me up. Sometimes I couldn't find him for days. I'd call the bars looking for him, and the on-duty bartender would stay true to John and say he hadn't seen him. I knew better. I would call the pay phone at the bar and ask for one of my girlfriends, who would confirm he was there drinking. At least I knew he was okay. I remember thinking at times, *This isn't right. What am I doing?* But then I would say to myself, "He's going to straighten up one day, and he's not going to do it with someone else after all the time I put in." So I stayed.

It was particularly bad when his mother, who I was very close with, was dying. We knew her death was imminent. John was on a bender, and I couldn't locate him. I remember feeling angry. I tried to help him "hide" his drinking from his family, but this time I couldn't. I told them I couldn't find him. It would become their responsibility to find him, and it would serve him right that they knew. My parents didn't like my relationship with John. They said it was because he wasn't Jewish. But I knew it was his drinking and his "irresponsibility." They could see the times I was upset, and they knew it was because of him.

At the time, I had no idea what Amy was thinking about our future. As far as I was concerned, my entire world was nocturnal—drinking, getting high, and sleeping it off.

CHAPTER 5

ROCK BOTTOM

I gotta get off, gonna get
Have to get off from this ride

—"THEME FROM *VALLEY OF THE DOLLS*,"
ANDRÉ AND DORY PREVIN (1967)

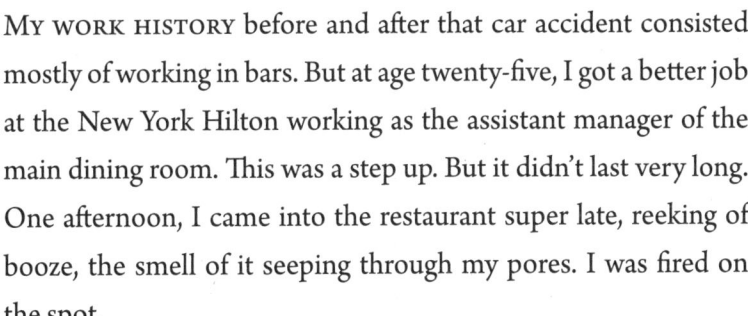

MY WORK HISTORY before and after that car accident consisted mostly of working in bars. But at age twenty-five, I got a better job at the New York Hilton working as the assistant manager of the main dining room. This was a step up. But it didn't last very long. One afternoon, I came into the restaurant super late, reeking of booze, the smell of it seeping through my pores. I was fired on the spot.

After that fiasco, I was back at the Midland, drinking as usual. It was like my home away from home, a place where I knew everyone, where I could just hang out to get drunk nightly. One night, I met one of the regulars at the bar, John Tarko, a big tough guy who had just gotten out of prison, having served thirty-nine months on a five-year sentence for the federal offense of stealing credit cards while working at the post office. John was 6'2" and a muscular 250 pounds, yet with a belly. He had enormous legs.

My father had once warned me there were two guys in the bar never to mess with—Tarko was one of them, Jack was the other. Jack was an exceedingly good-looking guy who personified the word *macho*. He was a badass. He was a former Golden Gloves boxer and a Vietnam vet. After he got out of the army, he became a window washer. He'd be perched up on those scaffolds in Manhattan, fifty, sixty, seventy stories high. He had balls of steel. And he was an intimidating guy who was very good with his fists. One night I saw him go off the handle and deck a few people at the Midland with a ferocious agility that was downright scary. Nobody messed with him. But he had a softer side too.

I have a vivid memory of Jack singing his rendition of "Reminiscing" by Little River Band, a soft romantic song. And Jack just nailed it. Women loved him. Seeing Jack in action, I admired him. He was about six years older than me, and in a lot of ways I wanted to *be* him because he was such a tough guy and did so well with women.

One night, when I was talking to Tarko, he mentioned that he just started his own furniture-moving business. He began with just one van. He didn't even have a license from the Department of Transportation to operate the truck. But he was forging ahead anyway. During the course of a very long night of drinking and listening to music, Tarko, who was five years older, impulsively said, "Come work for me. I need an extra guy."

It wasn't a question, it was a statement: "I'm gonna pick you up at four o'clock in the morning tomorrow to do a moving job. We have to be in Pennsylvania by eight in the morning, so be on time."

I shook my head yes. He agreed to pay me $10 an hour, which was good money back then, equivalent to $30 an hour today. I figured, *Why not?* I'd make some extra money and I liked hanging out with John anyway. It was this first move that bonded our relationship, I nearly blew it from the beginning.

I was *supposed* to be out front at my apartment at 4:00 a.m., but I never showed up. I got so drunk the night before that I blacked out and didn't even remember the conversation. That's how bad I was. Tarko was royally pissed. The following night at the Midland, he started ridiculing me in front of all the guys, verbally bashing the crap out of me: "What's the matter with you? You don't even show up for work!?"

In truth, I had a lot of pride in myself and generally had a good work ethic when it came to the bar. Ever since I was a teenager, I was always very willing to work. But alcohol was robbing me of any sense of responsibility. My drinking was at its all-time worst. As weeks passed, John was still relentlessly berating me at the Midland. Every night he would come into the bar and embarrass me in front of all the regulars. "Beyer is the guy who never shows up for work!" On and on.

One night, we wound up having an argument over the meaning of the word *perks*, which Tarko had used in a sentence.

And I asked, "What are perks?" I honestly didn't know what it meant but became defensive about it anyway. He started ridiculing me for not knowing what *perks* meant, like I was a dummy. And we wound up making a $100 bet as to whether or not somebody *else* in the bar would know the meaning of the word. I was naively convinced that nobody else would know it either. We decided to ask one of my regulars, a stockbroker named Bobby Ferone. He was a pretty sharp guy, but I sensed he wasn't going to know what the word *perks* meant. Sure enough, Ferone says, "What do you mean? Like, a percolator of coffee?" I laughed and I won the bet!

I would have been ecstatic except for the fact that John didn't actually *have* the hundred dollars to give me. Just like me, he was an alcoholic, all talk and, in this case, no money. So now, for the next couple of weeks, I was taunting him. "Hey Tarko, where's my hundred bucks? You're a deadbeat. You don't pay your debts." Now the shoe was on the other foot.

Since he couldn't pay up, I eventually approached him and proposed, "I'll make you a deal. If you never mention that I didn't show up for work again, I'll forget the hundred dollars," which was like $300 in today's money, a good chunk of change. He said, "You have a deal," and we shook on it. Thereafter, I started regularly working for John as a mover. And that's how I got into the moving business. It was a sheer accident, a fatalistic moment. As I think about it now, if John hadn't asked me to help him do a moving job, my life might have turned out quite differently. I owe him a lot.

Soon enough, I was showing up every day at 7:30 or 8:00 in the morning, sitting next to Tarko, the two of us doing jobs all over Long Island and Queens. As it turned out, I loved moving furniture. It was good, hard work; it paid all cash; and I had a natural affinity for it. No matter what the weight of the boxes or the furniture, I was big and strong, and I liked using my hands. I could size up a job, recognize the challenges and how to solve them. I also interacted well with the clients. Despite late nights at the bar, I still presented well: Like Mom always said, I always combed my hair and looked preppy and clean-cut even though I was drinking like a fish.

As a mover, I loved going into upscale neighborhoods and seeing all the new beautiful homes in places like Jericho or Garden City, Long Island. As a kid who grew up poor with parents who could barely get by, I was fascinated to see how the wealthy lived. And I always wondered if I would *ever* be able to live in a house worth $1 million or more. At this point, I was living in a basement apartment in Flushing. So how was I going to escape a blue-collar existence as a bartender/mover? I had no clue. But there was one thing I knew for sure: *I wanted to live a little better.* But how?

One day, Tarko, being a good soul, told me, "John, you're a smart guy. You should start your *own* moving company. We could work together and crowd out the competition. You could put an ad in alongside mine, which will lessen the chance of people calling somebody else. And we can do the jobs together and split the money." I wasn't sure. But he was. "We'll figure it out. Let's just *get* the jobs first."

In September of 1985, I placed my first ad in the *Penny Saver* classifieds. I named my company Man on the Move. My first truck had simple block lettering on it, with the letters as huge as they could possibly fit on the side of the truck. I was determined to get as much attention on the road as possible. Even in the parking lot, I wanted people to notice the truck. When negotiating with the gas station owner for how much I would pay him to park the truck on 214th Street and Northern Boulevard in Bayside, Queens, I had the wherewithal to insist that I wanted a spot on the very end of the row. I wanted that visibility. Somehow, even back then I instinctively knew the value of marketing.

About a year later, I changed the name to the plural *Men* on the Move because I wanted potential customers to understand that my company consisted of a crew rather than just me. John also wanted to present an image bigger than it actually was. His original company name, Man in a Van, was changed to Moving Ahead. No matter what the optics, the truth was that we shared a handful of the same dozen employees. This went on for years and it worked like a charm. Both of our businesses grew in spite of how much both of us were drinking. It was mind over matter. Yes, we got drunk at night. But we had a strong work ethic and we liked making money. So, we both worked as many hours a day as it took to get the job done, seven days a week.

But the drinking never stopped. I was depressed on the one hand and addicted to escaping that depression from the high I got from drinking. It was a huge mood swing back and forth. I felt up at night and down in the morning. Also, in terms of its impact on my future, I was getting tired of hearing the word *underachiever.*

Yes, I was surviving financially, working at the bar making a salary and tips, and making some money moving furniture, but there was a ceiling to what I could earn. I knew I had greater potential. I remember even saying to myself, *Maybe one day I'll own the bar—either the Midland or Murray Hill.*

By my twenties, I felt like I could run the whole thing. But for now, I was living on tips and on moving jobs whenever I could get them. There was nobody to rely on financially. I had to fend for myself, which was okay with me. In fact, my relationship with money from the onset was always about self-reliance. I was the one who had created my first job at Waldbaum's, and I was still doing it. And even though I was a "star" in the bar, entertaining the patrons and making friends, I felt dead-ended, like I wasn't going anywhere.

I continued to see my therapist, Ron. His office was in the Chanin Building at 122 East Forty-Second, right near where Trump had just built the Hyatt at 109. I remember that, after therapy, I would take the escalator up to the second floor of the Grand Hyatt to the hotel bar called Trumpets. It was an elegant wood-paneled bar that I found appealing, a definite step up from the bars in Queens. Going there for a drink in my early twenties made me feel like a big shot. Meanwhile, I wasted whatever money I earned by spending it at the bar or putting coke up my nose.

Can you imagine, I'm going to therapy and then *drinking* afterward. At Trumpets bar in the Grand Hyatt on Forty-Second

Street, a guy named Gabe was the bartender, who I knew from Flushing. I would put a $20 bill down on the bar and pay for my first drink, but that was it. Everything else that I drank was on the house. After having numerous Manhattans or Rémy Martin Stingers, I would then drive home, drunk. And later that night I'd hit some local bars, drinking a couple more before finally driving home.

Amy had become disgusted with me and couldn't take it anymore. As she remembers it, "I finally had enough and stopped looking for John at night (a year and a half or so after his mother died). I truly had enough and believed I needed to move on. At the time, I didn't realize I was enabling him, but it was time to stop. I was almost twenty-five and deserved better."

While Amy realized it was time to stop, I didn't. I was relentless. One night, while I was at the Midland drinking with Jack, he told me that he had done some heroin during his stint in Vietnam. Though I did not consider him an all-out addict, I knew that he did dabble in it from time to time. But much more than being a drug addict, John, in my opinion, was a bona fide straight-up alcoholic. He could work at his window-washing job and at the Midland as a bartender, but his behavior was erratic, and he would easily lose his temper when drunk.

His world and mine were about to collide. Jack often worked Sundays behind the bar at the Midland. On January 6, 1986, I remember he was drinking Anisette, a very syrupy sugary drink with a licorice taste. He drank way too much of it, at least a bottle and a half. That day, he decided to use a little heroin too. At some point after work that night, he died. Yes, this big tough young guy was gone in his thirties. It was a total shock. When I heard the news, I remember being devastated. How could this be? Jack was such a charismatic, warm person. It was impossible to think that he was gone.

At the wake, people were chattering away about drugs being the cause of Jack's death, saying, "It was the heroin, the heroin . . ." But I remember looking at them with wide eyes and wanting to scream at them, saying, "No, it *wasn't* the drugs!" Even though I was in the throes of my own alcoholism, I had some clarity and could separate out the true cause of Jack's death. In my mind, I knew it was the alcohol that ultimately killed him. If he had not had so much to drink, he wouldn't have done the heroin. And he'd be alive. I knew he died of alcoholism, just as my father had.

It was on that day that I began drinking even more, uncontrollably, going on a bender that lasted from January 6 to March 31, 1986. It was the bender of all benders. During that entire time, I barely drew a sober breath. I was drinking nonstop. I was having trouble even showing up for moving jobs. My birthday on February 4 was a total blur. I was just spinning out, unable to handle another death.

On March 31, 1986, I didn't wake up—I came to. I was dazed in bed, blinking my eyes repeatedly in order to even recognize my surroundings. I wasn't sure where I was. I stood up to look outside the window. I pulled back the blackout shade in my bedroom, peering out to see the time of day. I wasn't sure. The sky was a medium blue. The clock said 6:00, but I did not know if it was a.m. or p.m. Somehow, I gathered myself up and made it to the telephone. And for some reason, I called Alcoholics Anonymous.

Why did I do it on that particular day? As I would later learn, the First Step of Alcoholics Anonymous is: *We admitted we were powerless over alcohol—that our lives had become unmanageable.* For sure, my life *was* unmanageable. That's a kind way to put it. My life was a mess. When you wake up and the clock says six o'clock and you don't know if it's day or night, that's a pretty profound checklist item for whether you're an alcoholic. This was the bottom.

I was tired of being alone. I was tired of feeling less than— underperforming based on my real potential. I was tired of hiding what I was doing. I was tired of lying. I was tired of feeling sorry for myself. I was just tired of *being* sick and tired.

I knew about the program because my Uncle Andy (my dad's brother) had gotten sober in the program. As a sponsor and participant, he helped a lot of fellow addicts. I also heard about AA from my mother, who had tried the program a few different times in an attempt to get sober. She admitted she had a problem. But she never stuck with it. And it never stuck with her. In addition, my therapist, Ron, had years earlier suggested I go to AA. But I just never did it. You might say that I had not reached the point of desperation.

On that winter day, there I was, on the phone, the hotline operator telling me that there was a meeting in Bayside Hills that night. I jotted it down and stuffed the information in my pocket. Before I left the house, I had had a quick phone conversation with Amy. And I remember her concern.

"You've been MIA. Where have you been?"

I told her that I was going to an AA meeting that night. I made the commitment to do it.

"I'm going to get help."

And she seemed relieved. As she remembers that day,

I had stopped calling John. And I believe that my pulling away made a difference because, less than two weeks later, he called me to say that he was going to get help and that he was serious. Although I truly was "finished," how could I not support him? After all, having invested in the relationship for all this time, I couldn't let someone else reap the rewards. I *knew* his getting help was going to happen one day, and here it was. How could I abandon him?

On the same day, March 31, I happened to get a notice in the mail that my new library card was ready for pickup. Ron, my therapist, had years earlier suggested that I spend more time in the library back when I was majoring in English in college. Even in my hungover state, I decided to go to the library that day to sign for it. Getting ready to leave the house, I was a little shaky, red in the face, and bloated, so I got showered and changed. At about noon, I drove to the library, which was crowded and noisy that day. There were little school kids all running around. I had to wait in line to get my card, which I hated, so I was anxious to get out of there as soon as possible. In fact, I was thinking that when I left the library, I would head over to the local pub near my apartment to get something to eat. But I knew underneath that I was really going there to drink.

Finally, when I was leaving the library, I passed by a tall rack of books, but it was all the same book. The book instantly caught my eye. It was on the subject of DWI (Driving While Intoxicated). For some unknown reason, I was compelled to pick it up. As I stood there, I began thinking about the long saga of my car accidents, including the disaster that had led to the lawsuit and the scars on my face and the injuries of that woman. I also thought about a few other accidents I'd had while drunk. Although I constantly drove drunk, I was never arrested for a DWI. Back then, even when you were pulled over, the police, more often than not, just let you go with a warning.

As these thoughts were going through my mind, I opened the four-hundred-plus-page book inadvertently to the one exact page on the subject of AA. I stood there stunned as I read the one paragraph that ended with this sentence: *"Alcoholics Anonymous is the best treatment for the disease known as alcoholism."* There are no coincidences. To this day, I feel as if a higher power said, "This sick puppy has had enough. Let's push him in the right direction."

I closed the book and left. That night, I went to my very first AA meeting. When I entered my apartment, Amy was there making us dinner. My feelings at the conclusion of that first meeting remain vivid in my memory. Before the door closed behind me, I said to Amy, "Our entire lives are going to change."

CHAPTER 6

THE FIRST STEP

I can see clearly now the rain is gone
I can see all obstacles in my way
Gone are the dark clouds that had me blind
—"I CAN SEE CLEARLY NOW," JOHNNY NASH (1972)

FROM DAY ONE, I threw myself into the AA program. It gave me an entirely new focus on life. The routine was simple. No more bars. No more drinking. All I did was just work, not drink, and go to meetings as the AA program suggests.

The transformation from an active alcoholic to sobriety was quite rapid. I was as drunk as could be on March 29 and 30 of 1986. And the very next day when I went to my first meeting, I was already feeling better, recovering from a massive hangover. Even though I didn't understand it yet, I knew I was in the right place. It was life changing. I declared to Amy that we needed to change our lives and all our bar friends, the ones who drank. I couldn't be in the bar environment anymore. Amy said that she would stick with me and support me through this. So that was the end of many of her friendships. And she said it was okay.

"I felt relieved and validated," Amy remembers. "After all, I knew John well enough to know it would certainly happen. But it took me a while to trust him and believe that things had changed. It was an adjustment. When he told me that we needed to immediately change all of our friends, it was the end of many of *my* friendships too. But it was okay. I would stick with him and support him through this."

I will never forget the night I stepped through the door of Bayside Colonial Church in Queens and walked down the stairs to a small kitchen basement for my first AA. That first meeting was life changing. I found myself in the company of people who didn't drink alcohol—at all! I thought this was kind of odd. I really had no idea that there were millions out there who *didn't* drink on a daily basis. Coming from my background, with two alcoholic parents and a regular circle of friends and customers at the bar, I knew nothing else *but* heavy drinking. Night after night, it's all I ever saw. And it's all I ever did. Everybody drank.

Walking into a brightly lit room with sober people and a pot of coffee was like entering a new dimension. No music. No alcohol. It was eye-opening. I felt relieved to leave behind the bar culture that was destroying me.

I soon discovered AA meetings are a world unto themselves. Ninety percent of the time, they're held in church basements in your local community, any night of the week. In Queens and Long Island, where I was, you could either walk to a meeting if you wanted to or you could take a ten-minute drive and get there easily. I was very fortunate to have that kind of easy access. Once inside the room, I found that the meetings were made up of a very diverse crowd, men and women, young and old, rich and poor, and multiple ethnic, religious, and economic backgrounds. It was a total melting pot, just like the Midland Bar. I could see that the disease of alcoholism spared nobody.

At a meeting, you could be sitting next to a twenty-two-year-old recovering alcoholic who worked stocking shelves at your local drug store, and on your other side could be a sixty-three-year-old Wall Street executive making all kinds of money with a big house on a hill. And the younger guy might have more sobriety than the older one. And they would both bond and help each other. That is the beauty of recovery.

At my first meeting, which was designed for beginners, I was welcomed with open arms as we went around the room to introduce ourselves. There were about twenty-five of us. Like many churches, the one that rented space for the meeting had become neglected. The room needed paint. The folding chairs were uncomfortable. But the people, I noticed, seemed very comfortable—with themselves. Most of them raised their hands to introduce themselves one by one. "Hi, my name is Rose and I'm an alcoholic." In a chorus, everybody would respond, "Hi, Rose!" And then on to the next person. A few of the newcomers didn't want to name themselves as alcoholics just yet. They just passed. But I raised my hand right away that first night with no problem. "Hi, my name's John, and I'm an alcoholic."

From that first night onward, I met warm, loving, honest people who just wanted to help one another. It was a group effort because, as I learned, recovery from alcoholism cannot be done alone. It can't be done in isolation or through willpower. That's why the first word in the First Step of AA is *we*: We admitted we were powerless over alcohol—that our lives had become unmanageable. By the time I walked into the basement, my life was unraveling. I was out of control, my physical and mental health crashing. But from that first meeting in the church, I felt at home.

It was actually a huge relief that I didn't have to drink anymore. I felt so beat up from the struggle of drinking. Drinking is work. It's exhausting. It takes all your time. You're either on a binger, drinking toward a high, or collapsed in bed, attempting to recover from a hangover. It's a vicious cycle that will eventually kill you or somebody else. And now I felt free from it for the first time in years.

At this point, I *wanted* to change. I was done with drinking. I didn't want to die like all the people in my life who succumbed to alcoholism—my father and my mother and Jack and Jimmy. All those deaths were ultimately caused by alcohol addiction. And I didn't want that to be me. I found such comfort in the companionship of fellow alcoholics, this little group of people, a subset of society, who didn't drink. And *I* wanted to be one of *them*.

In fact, for me, getting sober wasn't a physical struggle. Some newcomers had withdrawal symptoms—loss of appetite, sweating profusely, shaking, nausea, headaches, or even delirium tremens or disorientation. But I had almost none of that. I'd say it took me just about a week to bounce back. I felt clear-headed and energized, and my mood was better too. I also looked less bloated and exhausted. I guess, at age twenty-six, I had youth on my side. Also, I was sweating everything out of my system with daily manual labor, moving furniture in and out of buildings, up and down stairs. It was a fantastic physical outlet. And not least important, working was a very good thing because it kept my time structured. I felt productive.

Other than AA, my life was all about Men on the Move. My typical routine: I would be out the door by 7:00 a.m. on my way to a moving job for a ten-hour day (or for as long as it took to get the job done). I would then come home, listen to messages on my answering machine, return phone calls, give estimates, then shower and change. Then I'd have a quick dinner and get myself to an AA meeting by 7 or 7:30 p.m.

I don't know what made me do it, but I went to a meeting almost every single day, over three hundred meetings that first year. And the more meetings I went to, the more I *wanted* to go. It was habit-forming in a good way and fulfilling. I heard others talk about their desperate need for alcohol and the escape it provides. I was learning that alcoholism is a progressive disease that brings you down, destroying your health, impacting your relationships, killing your career, worsening your finances, and wrecking your peace of mind. I could now see that every part of me was suffering when I walked into the program.

These people in the church basements had something that I wanted—sobriety. And just being in their presence was healing for me. I was destined to be in those rooms with sober people and to remain sober myself.

Immersing myself in the program was my top priority. I was ready and receptive. I threw myself into meetings with such fervor and intensity that it enabled me to build a true sense of spirituality and a strong foundation. I liked hearing people share about how they had turned their will over to a Higher Power to stay sober. They didn't want to hide or lie about things anymore. They wanted to live a more productive and satisfying life. And that's what I wanted too. I was tired of lying and cheating and being the chronic underachiever that I had become. I started living the AA model. Just don't drink and go to meetings.

As I would share in the rooms, I drank to escape *whatever* I was feeling at the time. I drank when I was happy because I wanted to feel happier. I drank when I was sad to numb the sadness or to snap out of it (though it made me even more melancholy). And I drank when I was even and calm. It just didn't make *any* difference. No matter *what* I was feeling, I was never comfortable in my own skin. And that's why I drank.

While it was easy for me to introduce myself and admit to being an alcoholic, I didn't share my deepest emotions or troubles during my first year of meetings. A lot of people entering twelve-step meetings are highly emotional. They cry and pour their hearts out. They really expose themselves. But I wasn't a big emotional sharer. Instead, I remained somewhat guarded, reluctant to reveal any of the most intimate things about my reaching bottom. My typical share was something like this: "Hi, my name is John. I'm an alcoholic. And I didn't drink today. I had a good day. I worked very hard on my moving job, the customer was happy, and I made some money, which allowed me to pay off some more of my debts. After the meeting tonight, I'm going to the diner with the guys. And I'm feeling pretty good right now. Thanks for letting me share."

During these early months of recovery, I remember so vividly a member of my group named Walter, a fifty-five-year-old clothing salesman who had been sober for decades, had been in AA for years, and was eager to mentor newcomers. To a twenty-six-year-old kid like me, he was like Moses, an icon revered by the AA community. People loved him. He spotted me, and I noticed that his eyes were so wide open that he looked like he'd just caught a fish. It was kind of weird. I could see the excitement in his expression, indicating that he wanted to help. He didn't exactly pounce on me, but as we had coffee after the meeting, he gave me a few suggestions. Simple things, like: *Don't drink and go to meetings . . . Try to do a 90 in 90: 90 meetings in 90 days . . . Get a sponsor . . . Stay busy . . .* And that's exactly what I set out to do. Walter ultimately became my first sponsor.

As I got deeper into the meetings, I learned that AA is filled with helpful slogans. "One Day at a Time;" "Easy Does It;" "Let Go and Let God;" "Keep It Simple;" "Progress, Not Perfection;" "First Things First;" "It Works *if* You Work It." One of my favorites was "Give It Away to Keep It." It's ironic that when you reach out to help another alcoholic, you really help yourself. That's how it works, one person doing service for the fellowship, which in turn keeps you sober.

Of course, nobody just quits drinking and suddenly feels better. It takes time and effort, and you go through mood changes during withdrawal, some restlessness and irritability and anxiety, which is why going to meetings is so therapeutic. You're around other people who have gone through the exact same thing.

One of the program suggestions is that a newcomer should get a sponsor—someone who is a senior member of the group who has been in recovery for at least a year. The idea is that a sponsor can help you navigate through the process of getting sober. A sponsor supports you on the phone, answers questions, and works with you on the twelve steps while also keeping you accountable. More than anything, you can confide intimate things to your sponsor that you may not be comfortable sharing at meetings.

Walter supported me. He encouraged me to attend as many meetings as I possibly could. He urged me along. "John," he'd say, "I'll be going to the Oakland Gardens meeting (held at Hollis Woods Community Church) on Tuesday. See you there." (It was not a suggestion.) And then that night he'd say, "Tomorrow night, I'll see you at the Little Neck–Douglaston meeting," directing me to the church in that town. And on Wednesday, Walter and all the regulars would sip their coffee at the end of the evening and say, "Okay, Thursday we're going back to Oakland Gardens, so see you there." And then on Thursday night it was, "I'll see you at the

Bayside Hills meeting, in Bayside, on Friday." And that's how it went. Day after day after day.

As was the custom, after the meetings we would all go out for fellowship, often to the nearby Scobee Diner, a Queens institution in Little Neck. We would all just sit there, having coffee or dinner and getting to know each other. We talked about our lives and our relationships and our jobs and career goals. We were bonding and supporting one another on a very human level with honesty and no judgment.

By attending meetings, I learned all about *The Big Book*, the four-hundred-page basic text of AA. It's the bible of the program, a best-selling book that has helped millions of people recover from alcoholism since it was published in 1939. It's just an amazing source of wisdom, describing all aspects of recovery—the original twelve steps—and the personal histories of the program's cofounders. Their stories have remained unchanged since the first edition, though new stories have also been added to the personal histories with each succeeding edition of the book.

Many of the meetings I attended would begin with a reading from *The Big Book*, frequently a portion from chapter 5 ("How It Works") or from chapter 3 ("More About Alcoholism"). In my mind, *The Big Book* should actually start with chapter 5. And later on, when I would work with a newcomer or sponsor a fellow alcoholic, I would always tell them to start reading *The Big Book* at chapter 5. I love how it begins, giving the reader hope: "Rarely have we seen a person fail who has thoroughly followed our path. Those who do not recover are people who cannot or will not completely give themselves to this simple program."

If there was hope for me, there was hope for everyone. As I learned, it's all about surrendering. But you have to have the willingness to do it.

Almost immediately after I started attending meetings, I wanted to spread the word about AA to all my friends at the bar and beyond. But as I learned from Tradition 11, AA is a program of attraction, not promotion. We don't sell it. You don't see AA advertisements. Anonymity is key. I didn't actively advertise. But honestly, it was a struggle watching my buddies from the bar, the guys I was working with on trucks, and my friends at the gas station too, all continuing to drink and ruin their health, including John Tarko. I did share with them how much AA was helping *me*. My getting sober became very attractive to all the guys I was working with, and they paid attention to it. In other words, I was glad to break my own anonymity to help them.

For example, the guys who owned the gas station where I rented a spot, Dave, Matty, and Ray, were all bona fide alcoholics. They were also hardworking, skilled mechanics who knew their craft and how to run a business. But they were all drunks. I wanted them to get sober. I wanted everyone to get sober. I was filled with gratitude and enthusiasm for the program.

I remember one day when it was about 90 degrees, Ray was passed out in the back of an old Chrysler Newport. It was so hot that his face looked like it was melting right into the vinyl of the backseat of the car. In previous times, he and I had done a little bit of drinking together at the bar after my moving truck would pull into his gas station. As I think about it now, almost every single one of the guys driving trucks were all heavy drinkers—and driving.

At first, as I told all these guys about my experience in AA, they looked at me like I had two heads, *"Who is this guy?"* But through the power of my example, I was getting through to a number of guys in my world who were actively drinking. I'm glad to say many of them started falling like dominoes, going to meetings and getting sober. Dave, Matty, and Ray all eventually joined the program and stopped drinking. So did John Tarko. None of them have had a drink in over thirty years. Perhaps my sobriety was the catalyst. But whether or not that's true is not important.

*   *   *   *   *

When it comes to anyone getting sober, you have to be ready. I never seriously considered drinking again. I saw how powerless I had been over my addiction, how it created such chaos in my life, such unmanageability. I recognized what a dumb kid I had been, how irresponsible I was. I was now showing up in the morning with more spring in my step. Everybody could see the immediate change in me. The phone would ring and I would answer it. I wasn't hiding. I was there. I was available. I was present. I was responsible. And my car was clean! My moving trucks had better equipment in them because I had money to buy more wardrobe boxes, blankets, and dollies. Sobriety was already providing my clients with better service. I was seizing each day with hunger and a sense of urgency.

If somebody called up and needed me to do a job immediately, I did it. And after a long day working, I often led beginners' meetings, which is part of doing service for the program.

My sisters were ecstatic with my sobriety, both relieved and proud, so glad that I had found the right help. Before getting sober, Denise and Cherie were always looking after me, taking me to the doctor and the psychologist, you name it. But now, there was no need to take on that maternal role anymore. They could see that I was taking much better care of *myself*, both physically and mentally. And because of it, I was leading a productive life.

Cherie was so ecstatic with my progress that she asked me to be her first son's godfather, so I was the one who presented him to the rabbi for his circumcision. In a way, I was becoming a *mensch*, a person with integrity and morality who was responsible. Suddenly, I was someone you could count on. I started to feel better about myself. I was able to look people in the eye. It's self-rewarding. The more responsible I was, the more responsible I became.

Amy was also thrilled with my sobriety and my progress. She reflects that,

> I no longer had to look for John in the middle of the night. Now, when he wasn't around, I knew he was at AA meetings or out to the diner with his new friends. I was still lonely, but it was different. When he *was* at home—he was *there*. He encouraged me to go to Al-Anon, but I wasn't the one with the problem and I was busy. I didn't go.

116

I eventually did try—not because of John's drinking but because of John Tarko's drinking. When my John was at his AA meetings, I would need to hunt John Tarko down at the bars to set up the next day's work with him. Maybe it was PTSD, but I wasn't going to go through this with him. I went to Al-Anon for a few months. But I wasn't comfortable there because everyone in the group had active alcoholics in their lives. Although the active alcoholic in my life, John Tarko, was the reason I went to Al-Anon, it depressed me too much. I didn't want to think back to the days of my John's drinking. Instead of reliving it, I wanted to forget about it. So, I stopped going to Al-Anon.

At my meetings, I was learning the principles of the program under Walter's guidance. While he was supportive, he was also somewhat controlling. I was a bit stubborn, trying to maintain a mind of my own. And after a period of two and a half months, it became clear that we didn't click. Walter was becoming critical of me because I wasn't following his instructions and program advice to the letter.

One day he said to me, "I think you're going to drink again. So, I don't want to sponsor you anymore." And with that statement, he just dropped me. I was furious with him. At this point, I had eighty-eight days of sobriety. As everybody in the program knows, a ninety-day benchmark is important, but Walter chose to detach from me just before this date. Although he walked away from me, *I* never walked away from the program or allowed his decision to stop me from going to meetings. I just kept going.

Looking back, I sometimes wonder if Walter "fired" me to actually *help* me stay sober by taking me down a notch. It's true that, in those early days, I was a little arrogant. You couldn't tell me what to do. And it's true that I wasn't listening to everything he said. But the one saving grace was that I wasn't drinking and I was going to meetings daily, which is the paramount thing to do. Anyway, after Walter predicted that I would go out and drink again, I took it as a challenge that I would *never* do that. And I never have had a drink since I entered the program.

Eventually, I did get another sponsor, Kevin, a thirty-four-year-old bookkeeper who was another one of the icons in the AA community. At the time I met him, he'd been going to meetings for four years. I got to know Kevin and appreciate his passion for sobriety in the program. He was relaxed, calm, and soothing. He just glowed. A very caring, warm person who was not judgmental. I referred to him as St. Kevin. I shared all my history with him, and he became someone that I totally counted on. In the early days, he listened to all my problems, me just venting. I talked about all the big stuff happening in my life, and he also listened to the bullshit, the broken shoelace stuff. In fact, over the last nearly forty years, he's helped me through many challenges. And I love him and his wife, Peggy, dearly. Kevin's a remarkable human being. He happens to have cerebral palsy, and a slight speech impediment, and he walks with a limp. But despite his health issues, Kevin, even back in his forties, managed to finish two marathons in under four hours. It's truly amazing. And when you ask him how he did it, he just says, "One step at a time."

During these early days together in AA, Kevin became an all-round pillar of support. I can still see us all standing together holding hands at the end of each meeting, saying the serenity prayer: *God, grant me the serenity to accept the things I cannot change, the courage to change the things I can, and the wisdom to know the difference.* I was beginning to see it.

As I learned, everybody worked their AA program differently. Some addicts in recovery make a lot of program phone calls in between meetings, but I tended to be more of an in-person type guy. Sometimes I would pick people up and drop them off at meetings, and we would sit in the car and talk. In the early days, I got to know a program friend named Jim Mahoney. He helped me tremendously. Jim used to work for the IRS, and he would joke all the time and say, "If your file ever crosses my desk, you're in deep trouble." He would always goof on me, which was fun. Or he'd joke, "I know you're getting paid in cash and not reporting it all." Then he'd say that he'd have to recuse himself from the case. I used to drive a very old '74 Dodge van that had a hard metal dashboard. I had magnets in the shape of a truck that advertised Men on the Move. One day, as I was in the car with Jim, my company was in its infancy and I had only one small moving van. He lined up an entire stack of magnets across my dashboard and said, "One day you're going to have a whole fleet of trucks, I can tell." He got to see that come true. He was such a lovely human being, but sadly, he died of cancer.

When I was sober only six months, Jim introduced me to the Matt Talbot Recovery Retreats in Sag Harbor at the Cormaria Retreat House. As I found out, going on a retreat offers recovering alcoholics the chance to seek a stronger spiritual experience and enhance their sober way of life. Over the years, I forged a strong and close relationship with Sister Ann Marino, who ran the Cormaria Retreat House for over forty years. Sister Ann was the soul of the retreat house. She was a sweet spiritual woman who welcomed all of us. Her loving, nonjudgmental way was healing. I carried those feelings with me each time I left the retreat and was able to tap into them as I needed.

I love those retreats. I go every fall and haven't missed one in thirty-seven years. There are always fifty to eighty guys who break down into little groups. And you hear the most honest and raw sharing there about things you might not otherwise hear at a typical twelve-step meeting. It is a common occurrence for attendees to confess their Fifth Steps there—more on the Fifth Step below. They talk about how they stole their mother's chemotherapy money to buy booze. They've even confessed to murder. In one case, one of the participants admitted he hit a guy with a baseball bat only to find out a year later that the guy had died. It was involuntary manslaughter, but he killed him. And I heard one guy talking about not only drinking but shooting up heroin and then sharing the needle with his wife. And his wife contracted HIV, got pregnant, and then passed the virus to the baby. To this day, he lives with unmitigated guilt, and he doesn't understand why he never got the virus but his wife and child did.

These are among the amazing stories you hear on a retreat, confessions from people that touch your heart. And the best part of it all is that everything is confidential and anonymous and safe. I've never heard any subject matter brought up in a retreat ever come back into the regular AA community. The retreat is a sanctuary, and everything said there is sacred. To respect that, I've even altered some of the details of these stories for privacy. Today, with gratitude, I sit on the board of the Cormaria Retreat House.

My therapist's reaction to my passionate new commitment to AA was somewhat mixed. As much as Ron profoundly helped me, he wasn't particularly pro AA, but he would be the first to acknowledge that AA saved my life and the lives of countless others.

As the first anniversary of my sobriety was approaching, I was encouraged by Kevin to do a so-called Fifth Step, which in AA is when you confess to another alcoholic all the things you've done in the past that have harmed yourself or others. As the step states, *Admitted to God, to oneself, and to another human being the exact nature of our wrongs.*

I learned, when you do a Fifth Step, you wind up talking about all the things you did that eat away at you and rent out space in your head. These are the demons that can even cause you to go back out and lose your sobriety. I knew that if I didn't do a Fifth Step with Kevin, I was going to drink again. (In that respect, Walter had been correct.)

In order to do Step Five, you have to let your guard down. You must be rigorously honest. And you must trust your sponsor completely. I felt that way about Kevin. I knew that everything I told him would stay completely confidential, that I could talk with him openly and honestly about all the intimate details of what I had done and how my behaviors had hurt myself and others. So, we talked about it all—what drove me to drink, my crazy (and sometimes illegal) behaviors under the influence, and the ways in which alcoholism had ravaged my life. First off, I told Kevin about all the lying, cheating, and stealing that had driven me to my bottom, about how I used to steal from my bosses by taking money from the register. I told him about how I had hit dozens of parked cars in a drunken state and then just drove away, taking no responsibility for it. I admitted the shame I felt about my car accidents, causing serious physical damage to people while driving drunk. This was a huge source of guilt for me, especially how I had hurt that elderly woman in the accident and then lied about it during the trial. I had also injured another woman pretty badly in a different car crash. But at the time, like many alcoholics, I took no responsibility for what I had done and just slipped out of it. I was in total denial. But by doing a Step Five with Kevin, I was finally facing up to it and making myself accountable.

I also talked about my relationship with Amy, how much I loved her but also how, at times, I had betrayed her trust. As I told Kevin, I had lied to her repeatedly about where I was and what I was doing at all times of the day and night. Like many alcoholics, I said whatever was most expedient to excuse my erratic behavior instead of revealing what I was up to. I lied about being faithful—when I wasn't—and I admitted to Kevin that I had been sexually promiscuous, even contracting an STD. All these were dark secrets, secrets that were part of the disease. In fact, I lied to *everybody* in my life, including my bosses, my two sisters, and my mother when she was still alive. It was layer upon layer of deception.

I even confessed to Kevin that when I was drunk in bed, I sometimes sat on the edge of the bed, thinking I was on the toilet bowl. Then, the next morning, I'd be so humiliated when I realized what I had done.

I also told Kevin about the physical damage I had done to my health: The scar on my face was a daily reminder of the car accident that had almost killed the older couple. I also told him about my stomach problems, about the gastroenterologist who had mistaken my X-rays for those of an eighty-year-old though I was only twenty-one at the time.

By the time I got all this off my chest, I felt relieved. It was cathartic to admit it all, even though it was a gruesome picture. Finally, the best part of doing Step Five was admitting all that I had done and being *grateful* that I had been given the gift of sobriety.

Having told Kevin everything about my past, I discovered that your past could still catch up to you. One day, for example, my moving buddy John Tarko introduced me to a barbershop not far from St. John's University, off Utopia Parkway. Angelo, the barber, was an old-school Italian who would give you the most incredible hot shave with the steaming towel. It was bliss. So relaxing. And Angelo was a master at it.

Here I was at the barbershop, years after the car accident and lawsuit, and I was sober now. Angelo had covered my eyes.

He was trimming my beard and shaving me. I could hear the sound of the razor against my skin.

"How you doing?" I said. He seemed upset because earlier in the day there had been a very bad traffic accident on the Long Island Expressway.

"It reminds me of an accident that happened here years ago," he said. And then he started recounting all the details from *my accident!*

I was beginning to sweat underneath the towel like never before. And as I heard the razor by my ear, I was thinking, *This is it. This is payback. Oh my God, he's gonna slit my throat. This is justice for what I did.*

Although I was asking questions about his memory of the accident, I was trying to be very cool about it. Angelo said that the husband in the accident, the plaintiff, was a customer of his! "The hurt people went to court for years and finally settled the case." He even knew the amount of the settlement. It was really eerie.

He then went on to tell me that when the couple got the money, the man ironically came into the barbershop drunk. He had been celebrating the settlement.

"Angelo, I'm rich. I'm rich," he said.

Knowing that they were happy with the settlement did help mitigate my guilt and remorse, which was profound. So this man's happiness actually brought some solace to me, some peace. They felt whole. Of course, I can see now that the settlement really wasn't enough money for all their pain and suffering. But as someone in their late twenties with immense guilt about what had happened, I felt somehow relieved that they had believed it was enough, even though the woman was hurt so badly. I came to learn later that this couple moved upstate and bought a retirement home. They both have since passed away.

At first, after that haircut, I didn't tell Angelo that I was the one who caused the accident. But a few visits later I did.

"See this scar that you've been carefully shaving around for years?" I asked him. "This was from a car accident that I had." And I proceeded to tell him that I was the driver of the car that hit his customer.

I remember that he stood there stunned, wide-eyed, and just kept repeating with his Italian accent, "You kidding me? You kidding me? You kidding me?"

Strange coincidence. To this day, I still have to carefully shave around that scar. Billy Joel wrote the lyric from the song "Pressure," "You have no scars on your face." But I do. I do.

CHAPTER 7

Beyond My Wildest Dreams

Dream on, Dream on, Dream on
Dream until your dreams come true
—"Dream On," Aerosmith (1973)

WITHOUT ALCOHOL, my life began to change in countless ways. I was more responsible. Suddenly, I had some money in my pocket and I was catching up on my bills, paying rent on time. I wasn't lying anymore to Amy or to my sisters about where I was or what I was doing. I was becoming more of a mensch. I didn't fully realize it at the time, but I was concurrently building a tremendous foundation of sobriety while creating a stable launchpad for my moving business. One thing helped the other.

I was entirely focused on both work and meetings. The idea of taking much time off for a vacation was an afterthought. I worked 360 days a year. I had so much energy that it felt as if I was shot out of a cannon. And even when I did take a short break, I would still work remotely from wherever I was, dialing into my answering machine and giving estimates over the phone.

During my first year of sobriety, I also felt motivated to catch up with all my friends. It seemed that The Group from high school were all achieving things—buying co-ops and condos—while I was stuck living in a dingy basement apartment. As I heard about their accomplishments, my competitive streak emerged and I felt driven to catch up to them. But it wasn't going to be easy.

By the time I got into AA in 1986, I was not only bottoming out on alcohol but was also in a financial hole. Between credit cards and the people that I owed money to, I was in debt for $7,000—equivalent to $19,000 today. To me, this was a huge sum of money. Amy would tell you that a lot of the responsibility fell on me. She helped me get my life back in order. She took over administering my bills and made deals with lenders. I would come home with the money from moving and I would say, "Here's the money. Please pay the bills." That action really set up the structure for how we've built our financial relationship. To this day, Amy administers all the financials. She keeps track of what comes in and what goes out. In sobriety, my relationship with money was once again changing. At an early age, from that first job herding shopping carts, I had learned that having money was empowering. And now I was able to recapture that feeling of

Mom and Dad's wedding, September 1950.

ABOVE: Denise, Cherie, and I on Christmas. Photo taken by Dad in 1963.

LEFT: Me at five years old. Dad took this picture, but shortly thereafter, he stopped taking many photos.

TOP: This photo was taken by my daughter Lauren in the back seat of a moving car in traffic. It stood on the Long Island Expressway for decades but came down only weeks after she took the picture. She also inspired, no, demanded, this book.

ABOVE: Amy and I on the couch in the senior office of John Bowne High School in Flushing Queens. This is where the meeting of the mind and heart began.

RIGHT: I am singing Barry Manilow in high school here. My Mom got to see me perform. Dad was a no show.

Top: The high school besties! Myself, Anita Rothberg, Bob Bellusci, Taryn Soba, Richie Chin, and of course, Amy Rice.

ABOVE LEFT: Amy and I at High school graduation, June 1978.

ABOVE RIGHT: With my parents at graduation. They had become very friendly even though they were both very much in the throes of their alcoholism. I was grateful they were there that day.

I started working at The Murray Hill Pub in Flushing where my mom used to drink. This was BEFORE my 18th birthday.

Just a year and a half later at the same bar from the previous picture. You can see the effects of drinking already taking its toll on me.

Partying with my Lefrak buddies Howie Stulberg, Richie Weintraub, and Steve Stulberg.

ABOVE: Cherie and Steve's
wedding June 6th, 1981!
My Dad barely made it there.
He died just a few months later
at the age of 56.

RIGHT: Amy and I married
on October 16th, 1987
at Terrace on the
Park of course.

TOP: I worked for months designing this to help bring awareness to the autism cause.

ABOVE: Lauren as an infant (1990) on the baby mat with those big brown eyes!

ABOVE RIGHT: One of my favorite pictures ever. The kids are so happy. Gregory is beaming and locked into the camera. Notice Amy's hand on his chest. Greg was what's known as a runner in the autism community. He would just take off and run. Amy has him firmly in place and told me later that his heart was pounding with excitement to meet Mickey!

Top: A great moment at Richie Weintraub's wedding July 13th, 2000. Jeff Lipton, Richie, Steve Stulberg, and myself.

Left: A photo of my father in law Larry Rice in 1998. I was showing him the space where I was about to build our self-storage facility. We had drained every nickel from every crevice to build this and borrowed even more. I remember him saying to me, "I really hope you know what you are doing." It turned out to be the best business decision I ever made and the financial bedrock and springboard for everything we did going forward.

Lauren playing soccer. She loved it, and I always say that I loved nothing more in my adult life than watching my daughter play soccer. She went on to become the starting middie as a freshman on the high school team and all county. She was competitive and enjoyed it as this picture illustrates so well.

RIGHT: Enter Patrick as he checks the right box and becomes Greg's counselor at Camp Huntington. This was about 2006.

BELOW: The gifted Keith Amerson visiting Greg at camp.

Richie Weintraub is sitting. He had already been diagnosed with ALS. He's surrounded by just some of the friends who rallied around him; just *part* of the village. From left to right is; Tony the barber, Jamie Pilero, myself, Karen Perri, Harry Hipper, Nancy Schneider, and Nuri Wernick.

Top: The proud dad walking Lauren, the beautiful bride
down the isle October 13th 2018.

Above: Nick Bardsley, Margaret Bardsley,
Mr and MRs Patrick Bardsley and Amy and I !!

ABOVE: A recent photo of Greg and Toni Ann. He's always happy to see her. Love those smiles!

RIGHT: My precious grandaughter Harper Bardsley.

Top: Love this pic! Almost all my nieces and nephews and their spouses at the Night in White Autism fundraiser supporting their cousin Greg. Left to right: Dustin Berger and his wife Gina, Jamie Berger with her sister Ashley Berger, Sara, who's married to Russel on the far right. On the far left are Elizabeth Kragic and Marko Kozul and then Greg with his sister Lauren. Missing (ugh) are Patrick Bardsley and Steven Freitas.

Above: Superbowl LVII in Arizona February 2023. Walter Silva, Rich Kianofsky, Bob Bellusci, Richie Chin, and myself. We had a blast.

ABOVE: Group Family photo taken at our home in 2024. This one has everyone in it!!

LEFT: Me at the piano, I really can't play (lol), but somehow I manage to create music.

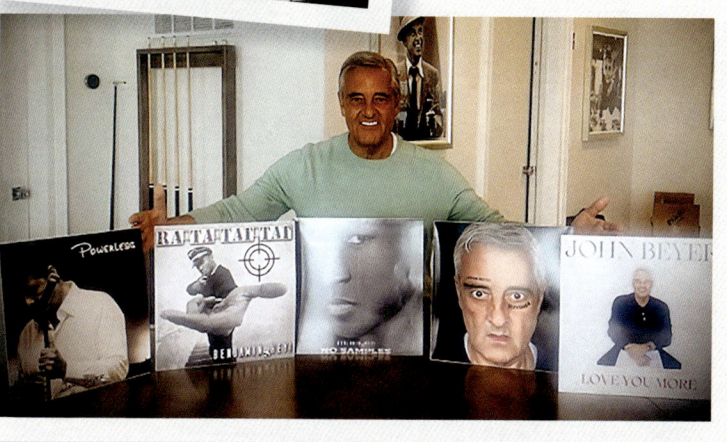

Me showing some of the music my collaborator Benjamin Hey! and I have created. I am proud of making "music that moves you."
www.JohnBeyerMusic.com

TOP: My beautiful sisters and I at Elizebeth and Marko's wedding Sept. 7th, 2024

LEFT: Lauren and I. She passionately, no, emphatically, encourages my music, the book, the play. Grateful for more than I can say!

Amy and I with our good friends John and Cathy Tarko. It's been over forty years since we started our moving companies. John and I were once told by someone in the industry that since we became competitors, we would never remain friends. That person could not have been more wrong.

Making wonderful family memories on the beautiful beaches of Aruba.

self-worth. Becoming financially responsible was one of the many gifts of sobriety.

Amy could see that I was a completely different person now because I was planning. I was motivated and I had vision. I was not just talking about things I wanted to accomplish, I was doing them. I was positive and upbeat. I was more caring and loving toward Amy than ever before. There wasn't any sneaking around anymore. I was responsible and dependable. I followed up on things that I wanted to learn instead of just talking about them. I would go and find out about things that I was curious about. For example, in my own industry, I wanted to learn how to move pianos. But I didn't know how it was done. Back then, there were no YouTube videos to show you how to move a baby grand piano.

One morning I drove around my neighborhood, literally looking for movers who were experts in this. I saw a large Mayflower tractor trailer with a grand piano out on the sidewalk. I told the guy, "I want to learn how to move pianos." He looked up at me and laughed. "Good, you want to help right now? Let's get started! Help us bring this baby up the stairs."

I was game. As I watched, they wrapped all the legs and pedals of the piano separately with moving blankets and tape. Then, with me helping, we all lifted the piano using lifting straps, and we placed the body of the piano on special dollies, a thing called a piano board, which I had never heard of. I then watched them lift and spin the piano at the top of the stairs. It was a very tight fit. And then they showed me the tricks of how you put all three legs on the piano and tilt it up onto its legs. There's a technique to it. After that tutorial, I started moving pianos myself. As I think back on it now, it was kind of fate that I had gone around my neighborhood just thinking about how to move a piano and instantly found those piano movers doing a job. The point is that I was interested in learning something new and expanding my business rather than sitting in a bar getting drunk. This curiosity never would have existed if I had still been drinking.

During this first momentous year of sobriety, Amy and I were living in two separate apartments. Three nights a week I'd stay at her place, while the other nights she'd stay at mine. That fall, we were upset when both of our landlords informed us that each was going to raise our rents. This was a wake-up call. Since we were essentially living together anyway, we decided to look for an apartment together. We found a beautiful two-bedroom on a tree-lined street in Bellerose, Queens, located along the border of Queens and Nassau County, Long Island. It was a bright, airy place on the second floor with a view of the trees and the sun streaming in. What a difference it was from the basement that I had been living in. The sunlight was like a metaphor for the way my life was now lighting up in sobriety. It seemed as if everything was rapidly changing for the better. By the end of the first year of sobriety, I was finally out of debt and steadily making money. And it was at this point that a major life event happened.

The new apartment in Bellerose was fine, except that it didn't have a refrigerator. There we were, moving our stuff in, when we realized we were going to have to go out and buy an appliance. Amy looked at me and said, "Who's paying for the refrigerator?"

At this point, we had separate checking accounts. I said, "We'll split it."

"But if this doesn't work out," Amy asked, "who gets to keep the refrigerator?"

"What do you mean, *If this doesn't work out*? Of course, it's going to work out. We're *going* to stay together."

Amy looked surprised. "What do you mean by that?"

I responded, "Well, we're going to get married." It seemed to me it was the natural course of events.

How weird that an informal proposal of marriage was prompted by the discussion of a refrigerator! I would have popped the question as a matter of course anyway, but that's the way it happened. It had always been clear to me that I was going to marry Amy. I had just never verbalized it. But I'm sure my intention to marry her was not surprising to her.

AA advises that you shouldn't make any major life changes during the first year of sobriety. Clearly, I didn't listen to all the rules—except for the not drinking part and going to meetings. But after nine months in the program sober, I decided that I was with the right girl, so why not? My sponsor, Kevin, sanctioned the engagement.

Amy had a very good job working at the European American Bank in Uniondale, Long Island, which had a beautiful waterfall in the lobby. For the holidays they would decorate lavishly with a huge tree and all kinds of Christmas decor. One evening just before Christmas, I met Amy there after work and suggested we take a walk. And that's when I proposed to her, underneath the waterfall of her office building. As for the ring, Amy's mom had died and had left behind a beautiful engagement ring. Since we didn't have any money to purchase a new ring, I had the stone reset. It was all ready to go for that night. Amy said yes, and we hugged and kissed. And she giggled because she said she knew it was coming. I could see that I had the ability to plan my future and make it a reality. When I proposed, I said to Amy, "There are two things that you need to know about me: One is that I am an alcoholic and that I intend to go to meetings for the rest of my life. Two, I am a restless soul, so hold on to your seat because it is going to be quiet a ride!"

On March 31, 1987, just three months later, I celebrated my very first sober anniversary in AA. I will always refer to this as the best night of my life. Managing to stay sober for a year, and not feeling like I was white-knuckling it, was liberating. I felt free. I wanted this. Staying sober wasn't a fight or a struggle for me. It was the opposite. I felt blessed.

At the meeting that night, as I got up to collect my one-year sobriety coin, I remember looking out at the people who were there to support me—all the familiar faces from my home AA group in the Bayside, Queens; my sponsor, Kevin; Amy; and, of course, very poignantly, my two sisters, Denise and Cherie, both so proud of me. My sisters knew, better than anyone, how far I had come. They had seen me in the depths of my addiction. And they had suffered through it themselves with the impact of both our parents dying of alcoholism. This turnaround in my life was a miracle for our family. There I was, recovering from a family disease that would have killed me. It amounted to a second chance at life.

That night, I remember saying to myself, *If you can stay sober a year, maybe you are worthy of having anything in life that you want.* I felt I could *be* and *have* and *do* anything I wanted in life. Before I stopped drinking, I felt like a caged animal. But now in sobriety, I was suddenly let out of the cage. I felt free and able to conquer anything I put my mind to. I wanted to put my paw prints all over the globe. And from that day forward, that's how I've been living my life, pushing forward and being productive, no longer weighed down by the past.

*   *   *   *   *

In 1987, when Men on the Move was in its infancy, Amy was still working at European American Bank as a benefits coordinator and administrator in charge of handling the 401(k) retirement plan for the bank. She was only twenty-six at the time and handling benefits for five thousand employees. It was a huge responsibility. To be that young and doing so well was impressive. She was making about $40,000, a very good salary, especially at twenty-six years old. Another big benefit of her job was that it included great health insurance benefits for both of us.

As Men on the Move grew, Amy was always a part of making it all work. As busy as she was at her full-time job, she also managed to create the back office for Men on the Move. Amy understood organization, filing, and accounting. Her father,

Larry, was a CPA, so the importance of keeping good records was ingrained into her.

As I learned, when you're in the moving business, you're highly regulated and you have to do filings with the Department of Transportation. I hate that stuff. To me, it's a bureaucratic waste of time. She helped me with all the required filings, which were time-consuming and complicated. Amy took the burden off me. As time went by, she willingly handled all the paperwork. She worked part-time and on weekends and in the evenings too. Her effort was incredible. We made a great team.

The company was growing quickly and making so much money that the paperwork was becoming a full-time job. Inevitably, the conversation with Amy became, "Should you leave the bank?" She would tell you that she had been thinking of it all along. And I tell you that I'm the one who initiated it and really pushed it.

In the midst of discussing this transition, I remember my sister Cherie reprimanding me, with her finger in my face. "How dare you suggest to Amy that she leave a secure job? You are making a mistake. You should not be doing this. You're giving up her benefits." It was a very challenging conversation.

Cherie's input always came from a good and caring place, so I didn't get angry. I simply responded, "Yeah, we're going to be able to pay for those benefits on our own."

I felt secure enough financially to encourage Amy to leave her job regardless of what Cherie thought. And that's what we decided to do: Amy left the bank and started answering the phones and booking moving jobs full-time. Even though moving wasn't her expertise, she was incredibly bright and picked up everything very quickly.

In fact, she single-handedly created what we call the Blue Sheet, the intake form that we use to book jobs over the phone, earning its name because it's handwritten in blue ink by us. It includes the date of move requested, the pick-up and drop-off addresses, questions about the amount of furniture and other delicate items that required special packing, the number of boxes, cartons, and wardrobes needed, you name it, plus a question about how they heard about us. On the back of the form was a detailed checklist of the client's furniture to be moved.

Amy actually created the Blue Sheet while she was still working at the bank. In fact, she used their Xerox machine to make multiple copies of the forms and then smuggle them home. Thirty-seven years later, we're still using that same sheet for the initial phone intake. And unlike many companies, we still write up the information rather than entering it directly into the computer. This is a more accurate and thorough way of doing it.

Bottom line, Amy created the entire corporate structure for the back end of the business, while I was on the front end, out there getting work and promoting Men on the Move. In terms of her leaving the bank, it was a seamless segue. We didn't pay her a salary but just took money from the business as we needed it to cover our expenses. We never felt the financial loss of Amy giving up her job because her presence at Men on the Move made up for it right away, catapulting us to the next level. She's been next to me at the helm of the business ever since.

Ultimately, another added plus of Amy working from home would be her ability to have more time to take care of our children. In our scrapbooks, there are a couple of great photos of Amy talking on the phone to a client while rocking Lauren at the same time. That was Amy—incredibly capable, efficient, and thorough, almost to a fault.

In fact, if anyone asked me about my secret weapon in business or in life, it would be Amy. I am forever grateful for the day I met her. She is a great mother, grandmother, and wife, a true heroine in every sense of the word, which is why I dedicated the book to her.

*   *   *   *   *

Amy was still at the bank in her full-time job when we started planning our wedding. In planning for our wedding, we didn't have a lot of money. With my mom and dad gone and Amy's mother deceased, we had to pay for the wedding on our own. Amy's dad, Larry, was alive at the time, but he had remarried a woman who was overly possessive of him, resenting any interaction that Amy had with her dad, and he went along with whatever his wife told him to do, even though he had always doted on Amy, who was his only child. This was incredibly painful for Amy. One time, after trying to get a message to her own father but being blocked by the wife, Amy collapsed in my arms, sobbing like I've never seen before or since. But Larry's new wife just didn't want anything to do with Amy, so the feeling became mutual. And because Larry was not very supportive of our engagement, Amy's relationship with him fell completely apart. They didn't speak for a long time. So, in effect, with three of our parents dead and Larry estranged, we had no parents in our lives at all.

Although Amy had a good job and I was working like a maniac, we still didn't have enough disposable income for a wedding. By this point, as I said, I had finished paying off all my debts and was now saving up. As Amy remembers it, "As part of my continued focus on clearing up John's finances, I now needed to create a new pot of money, a joint account set up just for our wedding. John gave me everything he earned (minus, I presume, spending money he needed for lunch), and I paid his bills and saved money for the wedding."

But then, because I felt I needed to expand my business, I actually took all the money we had saved, $3,500, out of our wedding account to buy a new *truck*! That night, when I told Amy what I had done, she wasn't too happy to say the least.

"How did I react?" she recalls. "I took myself to the Midland Bar to drink! Who did I run into? John Tarko! He was still actively drinking, so it wasn't surprising that I would see him there. After his initial surprise at seeing me there, and after I told him how upset I was about John buying the truck, he said, 'Best thing he's ever done—you'll see, it's going to change your life!' 'Sure,' I said, 'if I want to get married in a truck!'"

But John Tarko turned out to be right, because that truck enabled me to book more work and do bigger jobs, which allowed me to exponentially expand my business and ultimately make much more money. I quickly replaced that $3,500.

The venue we chose for our wedding is called Terrace on the Park, a well-known banquet hall located in Flushing Meadows Corona Park in Queens, the site of the 1964 World's Fair. Years earlier, I briefly worked at Terrace before I was fired for being drunk. It was ironic that I was now sober and returning as a customer, not an employee.

A lot of my friends worked at Terrace, so I knew they would treat us well. But it was going to be expensive, and I committed to having our wedding there before we had the money. We put down deposits, but it was going to be a photo finish to see if we would make it to the finish line. We committed to a big wedding and a honeymoon to Hawaii. I told myself, since the wedding was ten months away, I was going to work like mad, sixty, seventy, sometimes even eighty to ninety hours a week! Amy thought I was a little crazy. But together, we made it happen. When you're putting in those kinds of hours, you're going to make money. Plus, I knew that we would be getting wedding gifts too, which would help defray the costs.

October 16, 1987, was a beautiful, clear day. On the guest list were all our closest friends from high school, including Bob Bellusci, who had introduced Amy and I in the first place. He was my best man. Taryn was Amy's maid of honor. Also, from The Group there was Richie Chin, Anita Rothberg, and Walter Silva. We also invited my good friend Alan Weinman. Plus, we had Amy's two first cousins from California, Elise and Lori Foreman. My two sisters walked me down the aisle. It felt great. And they both looked stunning. Amy, who looked adorable, was walked down the aisle by her paternal uncle Hal (Amy's own father did not attend).

When reflecting on our wedding, Amy said, "I was happy and proud at our wedding. We did this all on our own! Even our Midland Bar friends, who we started to move away from, were there, as we cared about them and they cared about us."

That day, I don't know why, but I was suddenly very nervous during the ceremony. And I'm not a nervous type. And even though I never sweat, I was sweating that day. It's kind of funny. In the wedding video, you can see Bob patting me on the back to calm me down, as if to say, "Take it easy, boy." I guess I was anxious because I knew that getting married is a *big* deal. It's like, there's no going back now. You can't change it. As for Amy, I think she loved it. And she made a beautiful bride.

Behind the scenes that day of the wedding, my childhood friend, Richie Weintraub, was indispensable. Richie was one of the catering managers at Terrace, but he wasn't working that day because he was a guest at our wedding.

On our wedding day, Richie came over to give me a big congratulatory hug. And then he said, "Let's go in the dining room and take a peek so you can see how beautiful the room looks." When we entered, Richie could see my face drop. I never was much of a poker player.

"What's the matter? he asked.

"Nothing," I say glumly, but it was obvious that I was not happy.

"No, really? What is it?" asked Richie

Prior to the wedding, I requested that the room be lit by elegant votive candles, but on all the tables were lavish, glitzy Liberace-style candelabras. It was just awful. The cocktail hour was going on in the other room and I just assumed I was going to have to live with the ugly centerpieces because it was too late to change them.

I walked back to the cocktail reception disappointed but thinking to myself, *How important is it anyway?* Less than five minutes later, Richie dramatically pulled back the curtains for the guests to walk into dinner and to expose the beautiful dining room with the votive candles elegantly illuminating the room. There wasn't a candelabra in sight! I don't know how he got it accomplished that quickly. It was almost as if Barbara Eden from *I Dream of Jeannie* had just blinked her eyes and nodded her head and made the change. That moment is a great memory of both my wedding and my friendship with Richie. He later told me that he rallied up ten waiters and that they got it done in literally two to three minutes.

It was an unforgettable night. As Amy says,

I remember deciding on our wedding song. John wanted "Hard to Say I'm Sorry" by Chicago (my all-time favorite band). The song ends with the line, "You're gonna be the lucky one." John wanted *that* to be the message. But my choice was "Through the Years" by Kenny Rogers. After all that we had been through, all the pain and suffering that got us to this happy day, how could "Through the Years" not be our wedding song? And so it was. "And I'm so glad I stayed right here with you ... through the years ... when everything went wrong, together we were strong . . ." Little did we know just how appropriate that song would continue to be as we faced all that was still to come in our married life.

The stock market crashed on the Monday following our wedding (Black Monday, 1987). We were having our first honeymoon breakfast in Hawaii at the Hyatt Hotel when the news broke across the TV. So aside from the typical honeymoon memories, we had to decide if the $12,000 that we received as wedding gifts and that we left with our good friends should be invested while the market was low. Always thinking practically. It was all we had, so ultimately, we did not invest. Instead, we enjoyed our honeymoon and made wonderful memories.

On the day after we arrived at the Hyatt hotel, I remember that we took a drive on Hawaii's magnificent coastal road to Hana, one of the world's most scenic routes imaginable. It's a sixty-four-mile road on Maui that connects the towns of Kahului and Hana. The sights along the way include dense rainforests, waterfalls, lava tubes, colorful tropical flowers, and perfect beaches.

We were driving up this very narrow, dangerous road with

beautiful storybook waterfalls off to the right. But to the left of us was a steep cliff; a slight mistake would have taken us over the edge. It was a little scary. But I was already a pretty seasoned driver. At one point, with those tempting waterfalls on our right, Amy and I decided to just pull off the side of the road and go skinny dipping in a beautiful blue lagoon. It was filled with exotic flowers that were floating on top of the water. It seemed private so we felt safe taking off all our clothes and taking a very romantic swim.

It was like a scene from *The Blue Lagoon*, two twenty-something-year-olds in love naked in the water. We weren't having sex, but we were having fun. Suddenly we heard car doors slamming as a family of four pulled off to the side of the road. We looked up at the top of the cliff and could see them coming down the hill toward the lagoon! The two of us had to scramble out of the water *fast* to put our bathing suits on.

The next day, we were alone in our room being intimate. And at one point, we went out onto the terrace to continue our lovemaking. But we were interrupted when we looked up and saw a man on the very next terrace above us just leaning over, looking in the other direction. We had to crawl back into the room *fast* so that we wouldn't be seen. It was hilarious. Once again, we were laughing and joking around. It was great.

As newlyweds sometimes do, we wound up taking intimate pictures of ourselves. This was long before the days of digital cameras or cell phones, so you had to get the film developed. A few days later, we went to a shopping mall and dropped off the film at a store that promised "Prints to-go in 1 hour." Then we walked around the mall and had lunch. Afterward, we headed back to the film shop and saw that they had their photo developing machine in the front window. And there, for everyone to see, were vivid color pictures of us having sex coming down the conveyor belt! We were standing in front of that shop, hysterical with laughter, trying to contain ourselves, hoping that nobody else would walk up to the front window before we went in and got the pictures. It was a lot of fun.

*   *   *   *   *

Once we got back home from Hawaii, Amy repeatedly said that she wanted to start a family. That was my vision too. At this point, we were living in our nice, sunny apartment in Bellerose. But I told Amy that I didn't want to have a baby until we owned a house. In my mind, that was the order in which to do things, to make sure that we were on a path of financial stability. (Amy felt somewhat differently: "I've never been the risk taker. If John didn't push me through things, I'd probably still be in our two-bedroom apartment! But he meant it. He wanted to buy.")

I was excited. Everything in life was moving fast—a new wife, a growing business, the benefits of sobriety, and now the plan of having children too. It was a lot. But I was up for it. Even though I was only twenty-seven, the changes in me were profound. I had become a serious, motivated person. I was responsible. I was a hard worker. And I wanted to make this new life with Amy.

We started saving money to buy a home. As I mentioned,

I was feeling competitive and jealous of some of my friends who were all buying co-ops and homes. I wanted to catch up to them and excel too. Even hard-drinking John Tarko had bought a house. And he was really encouraging me to buy one too. I figured if all these people could buy a house, so could I. With John Tarko's guidance, Amy and I pushed ahead, scouring listings and seeing properties. In order to afford a house, we scrimped and saved. I wound up borrowing money from one of my sisters while Amy borrowed more from her uncle, which allowed us to finally buy our first house in New Hyde Park, Long Island. It was a Cape Cod–style house, a tiny, rectangular, one-and-a-half-story place. It was so small that, as John Tarko joked, "You would have to go outside to change your mind." The price was $205,000, which was a lot of money then. (I think I may have overpaid, because we sold it for less a few years later.)

I remember the closing being very nerve-wracking. It was scary. I even got dressed up with a suit and tie. We were signing and committing to repaying all this money. We were so nervous and thinking, *Are we going to be able to afford this?*

To get to the closing, we needed to pull money from anywhere we could. I had to be creative to make it happen. I found a way. Afterward, we came home and were completely drained. We took off our clothes and lay down. And I said to Amy, "Okay, now we can make a baby!" Well, we tried. It didn't happen at that very moment, but it was fun trying!

The moving date into the new house was April 20, 1989, a key date I purposefully chose. I started my story with my move to

LeFrak City on April 20, 1968. That move had a profound effect on me. I chose that date, twenty-one years later, as my moving date because it is a day that stands for new beginnings for me. I would move yet again on April 20 in years to come.

I have to say that I felt a huge sense of accomplishment moving into a house of our own. I had taken all the positive steps in my life in sobriety—getting married, buying a house, owning a business, being a responsible man in every way that I could think of. I had just turned twenty-nine, and with three years of sobriety, I was feeling legitimate, like a real grown-up.

About five months after we moved into the house, Amy got pregnant.

I can never forget those early days of her pregnancy. Amy threw up so much that it became a regular part of my life. I would walk down the hallway and hear the vomiting from outside the bathroom door. And I couldn't believe that somebody was throwing up that violently. Sometimes, worrying, I would look through the crack of the door to confirm that she was throwing up instead of something much worse. It was terrible that she was that sick, though she got better as time passed. As Amy remembers it,

I didn't like being pregnant. I was *very* sick for the first three months. It was so bad that John and I talked about terminating the pregnancy. "I can't go through this again," I told him in anticipation of knowing we would want more than one baby. I had been an only child, and there was no way *my* child would be an only child. Yet I could barely get out of bed each day. John was out working on the trucks, and I would do my best to answer phones, do the book work, and set up the next day's dispatch with John Tarko. One day, when I was feeling especially sick, I told Tarko, "I feel like such a wimp. I can't believe this is me." Macho John's response: "Amy, think about what your body is doing. You're manufacturing a baby. *I* can't do that!"

The doctor assured us that despite Amy's severe nausea, her pregnancy was normal. It certainly seemed as if the baby was healthy and energetic. In fact, one indelible memory about Amy's pregnancy was that the baby was relentlessly kicking. It was crazy.

As you looked at Amy's stomach, you could literally see the indentations in her skin as the baby pushed her feet against her. We joked that it was an alien. We nicknamed the baby Pelé, after the great Brazilian footballer. And it turned out that our daughter one day would wind up becoming an all-county soccer player in high school.

By the time Amy was nearly nine months pregnant, she was still working in our basement, booking moving jobs and doing the paperwork. At this point, I insisted that she just couldn't do everything for the business once the baby came. So she agreed to hire some part-time office help—someone for two days a week to answer phones and help in our basement office. That was the start of our business growing beyond just Amy and myself.

"A few days before the baby was born, the permanence of what was about to happen hit me," recalls Amy. "I said to John, 'Do you realize that, very soon, we are going to have a new little person with their own little personality in our lives forever?!'"

And then, in what seemed a flash, there we were on Amy's delivery day. I remember that Amy pushed and pushed and pushed, trying her best to deliver, but she wound up having a caesarean instead. Believe it or not, the doctors let me into the room while they were performing the operation. And through the reflection of the medicine cabinet across the room, I was able to see clearly as they made the incision into Amy's stomach. I then watched as the doctors and nurses pulled the baby out and cut the cord. And so, on March 26, 1990, our baby, whom we named Lauren Beyer, was brought into our world. Once they handed the baby to me, the first thing I remember is that Lauren's bright brown curious eyes were so wide open, looking right at me, taking in the entire world.

Having a baby was wonderful. Lauren was so beautiful. We had created a child, an extension of ourselves and our love for each other. And I relished taking care of her. In fact, I was far from being one of those dads who refused to change a diaper. I was willing to do *everything*. But my wife, who's a control freak, actually wanted to do it all herself. I'd have to fight with her to change a diaper.

"Let *me* do it."

"No," she'd counter. "No, I got it."

Amy wanted to be perfect at it. "At the same time I had the baby, we were trying to grow our own business, so I put Lauren in a little bouncy chair and would rock her with my foot while answering phones and typing work orders. Because she was so regimented in her nap and feeding schedule, I could always predict when it was time to wrap up, take a break, and get her bottle ready."

For me, just holding the baby was special. During the night in the beginning, Lauren wouldn't sleep and would start crying. That drove us a little crazy. The crying wasn't as prolonged or intense as a baby who has colic, but Lauren did keep us up. Other than that, it was smooth sailing. She was a great little girl. And she developed quite a distinct personality right away. She was physically very energetic and active, a bit of a wiseass, a little devil. As Amy would describe it, "Lauren had a snarky and independent personality from the get-go. One of the young mothers in the neighborhood once told me, 'Lauren will one day give my daughter her first cigarette!'"

Even as a toddler, she was daring, always pushing the envelope, jumping from here to there with the joy that only a child feels.

"Unlike some parents, we didn't put up gates by the stairs or bumpers on the corners of tables," says Amy. "We believed Lauren should learn how to manage and maneuver because we might not always be right there to help her manage unfamiliar circumstances. We taught her at an early age how to go up and down the stairs. She learned how to duck under tables safely to get her toys and not bump her head."

Throughout her life, we've tried to teach Lauren to be independent and confident and to take risks. She picked that up at a very early age and has been that way ever since. When she'd get into trouble, Amy's friend would say, "You taught her to be this way. This is what you wanted." And I'd say, "Yes, and I am proud!" As a father, I welcomed the opportunity to create a good life for her.

She would become very athletic, but Lauren was feminine as well. While her grades were just okay, her athletic ability was off the charts, soccer being her main sport. (All that kicking as a baby paid off.) But she was good in lacrosse and basketball too, so she participated on all three of those teams. As a former basketball player, I wound up coaching her for a couple of years in her CYO (Catholic Youth Organization) league.

Although one baby was a lot of work, we still wanted more. About a year later, Amy got pregnant again. This time Amy wasn't as violently nauseous. Everything seemed to be going perfectly. Every one of the check-ups was right on point. But during her labor, Amy again had difficulty having a vaginal delivery. (I always wondered later if she felt guilty about that or felt as if she had somehow failed.) She tried extra hard, did her best, but the baby just would not descend. Again, she had to have another caesarian delivery.

That day, during the operation, I was feeling very frustrated. It seemed as if Amy's doctor was not being as attentive as he could have been. That's because he was making two deliveries at once, with another caesarian right next door. It didn't seem as if Amy was getting all his attention. But the operation did go smoothly, and our son, Gregory James, was born on November 29, 1991.

Everything seemed to be perfect. Our new baby was beautiful. I mean, stunning. (Being unobjective, ha ha, both our kids are very good-looking.) And from all signs over the next twenty-four months, Gregory was a very healthy, happy baby who seemed to be developing normally. All was well in our world with my wife, two children, and a thriving business. It seemed nothing could go wrong. Everything was going according to plan. This idyllic time of our lives reminds me of the lyrics of the Crosby, Stills, Nash, and Young song, "Our House." We had a very fine house with two kids in the yard.

CHAPTER 8

Not Quite as Planned

I believe the children are our future
Teach them well and let them lead the way

—"The Greatest Love of All"
by Michael Masser and Linda Creed (1977)

At age two, Gregory got all the standard vaccines for diphtheria, tetanus, pertussis, and poliovirus. He was also given shots for MMR—measles, mumps, and rubella. It was all supposed to be standard and drama-free. But in spring of 1993, the MMR test sparked a major allergic reaction for Gregory. He got violently ill and threw up profusely.

I remember that he literally drenched his stroller with vomit. (I had to hose it down outdoors.) He also had a high fever. It was very worrisome, as our daughter had never had any such reaction. But then, a short time after, Gregory fully recovered from this episode, with his temperature back to normal. Yet I noticed something different about him. He seemed quieter and was less responsive to our touching him or talking to him. He seemed out of it, like he was kind of dazed. But I figured it might be a lingering aftereffect from the allergic reaction.

However, one of our good friends, Taryn's husband, Richie Kianofsky, a computer systems analyst, felt differently about what was going on. One day, after spending a long afternoon at our home, he said to us, "John, Amy, there's something not right with Gregory. It doesn't seem like he's reacting to his name the way he used to." As the next few days passed, we started paying more attention to it. And yes, it was true that Gregory wasn't looking up or responding in the way he had been. No matter how we tried to engage him, he just wouldn't look at us in the eye. Nor was he responding to his name. Even year later, as I remember back to that day, it's still a very painful memory.

I felt there was a logical explanation for this, figuring that the problem with Gregory might be his hearing. We made an appointment to take him to the North Shore Community Hospital in Manhasset, Long Island. There, in the waiting room, I remember praying and hoping that Gregory's lack of respon-siveness was *only* because there was something wrong with his hearing. Amy was kind of annoyed by this because she didn't yet believe that was the issue. True, even as I was saying it, I sensed that the problem *wasn't* his hearing. And the hearing test turned out to be perfectly normal. When I heard this news, my chest got heavy. I was instantly disappointed and upset. If it *had* been his hearing, that would have been something we could have worked with and possibly improved. But if it wasn't that, I assumed the issue was *in his brain*, not so easily improved with hearing aids. As all this was spinning through my head, the hearing doctor at North Shore suggested that we next see a neurologist or a psychologist.

Over the next weeks, as we considered what to do, it seemed as if our son was disappearing before our eyes. Physically, he was still fine, from outward appearances a beautiful, healthy boy. But mentally he was even more remote. Suddenly, he could no longer respond to his name *at all*. And eye contact had disappeared too. It felt to me as if he just didn't want to interact with any of us or to participate with the rest of the human race. From months earlier, he had gone from acting completely fine to being shut down, closing his eyes on us. He wouldn't come close or look at us. I remember literally being face-to-face with him and he would dart his eyes away to avoid looking at my face no matter what. We were inches apart, yet he was miles away. It was a total disconnect.

On December 15, 1993, we next took Greg for further testing on Long Island to a PhD psychologist named Dr. Marian Solomon. She asked us to fill out a screening questionnaire, which summarized typical developmental milestones that most children reach by age two.

How was Greg playing, speaking, behaving, and moving? For example, by age two, a child usually notices when others are hurt or upset; or points to things in a book when you ask questions; or says at least two words together, like "More milk"; or points to at least two body parts when you ask him to show you;

or holds something in one hand while using the other hand; or tries to use switches, knobs, or buttons on a toy; or kicks a ball, runs, or eats with a spoon. Greg had been able to do a number of these things before, but no longer.

After studying our completed questionnaire answers and considering our description of the startling change in Greg's behavior, Dr. Solomon gave us a tentative diagnosis. "The lack of eye contact is a red flag. I think your son *may* have autism spectrum disorder [ASD]." ASD was defined, she said, as "a neurological and developmental condition that affects how children interact with others, communicate, learn, and behave." When I heard these words, I felt crushed. Autistic? It was like being thrown off a cliff. My brain was on fire. In an instant, the vision of our son's future consumed me. My mind was bombarded with a thousand questions: *What was going to happen to Gregory in the future? Would he ever be able to communicate with us again? Would he attend a typical school? Was he ever going to play Little League? Would he ever have a girlfriend or be able to drive? Could he ever become independent as he got older? Could he in any way lead a normal life?* All this was racing through my mind.

After the appointment, as we walked out of the office building toward the parking lot, my eyes filled with tears as I held Greg's little hand. In that moment, I knew we were in big trouble, that Greg's medical diagnosis was going to require a lot of time, energy, and money. But most important, it was potentially tragic for Greg to have this diagnosis. That fact was number one in my mind. I knew that our lives had just changed forever.

As we got into the car, Amy was very quiet, at least not visibly upset. I think she was numb. Or maybe she was confused or didn't totally take in how serious it was. She didn't seem to quite get it completely. Maybe her calm reaction was a sign of self-preservation, cushioning the blow. But I knew that she would eventually come to understand and accept what was happening. As Amy remembers it,

> When we received Gregory's diagnosis, our world stopped. I felt paralyzed. In the days afterward, I couldn't focus on Lauren and I felt helpless with Gregory. Thankfully, my dad and I had reconciled by this point, and he was living with us. (He had broken up with his wife and had no place to go.) And he jumped right in to keep Lauren's world steady. He got her up and dressed in the morning, made her breakfast, took her to preschool. He knew her routines and she loved him. She would be okay.

Both of us would be always grateful to Larry, Amy's father, for how he stepped up during that period and really helped take some of the stress off of Amy and me. And, of course, we were also grateful to Richie K. for being brave enough to tell us that he thought something was wrong with Greg.

After that tentative diagnosis from the psychologist, we reached out to family and to our closest friends, though we didn't know what to say, much less what to do. What could we do to fix it? Who could we turn to? We didn't even know what first steps there were to take. Of course, we tried to find some information and resources about autism. But as we would discover, there wasn't much readily available. It wasn't like now, where you can google *autism* and get everything you need from every top source in the world. (Google wasn't even founded until 1998.) So, compared to today's standard of care, much of what we found might be considered inaccurate or outdated, and accessing the information was, to say the least, arduous.

On the night we received Greg's diagnosis, I went to my regular AA meeting at the church in Little Neck Douglaston, the place I'd been going to for seven years. I remember that there were about a dozen people in the beautiful wood-paneled room, mostly familiar faces with just a few people I didn't recognize. As I sat down, I felt lost and confused, just totally dazed. And naturally, I shared about what had happened earlier that day. As fate would have it, a guy named Rob came came directly up to me after the meeting and said, "John, it was good hearing you. I have an idea of what you and your wife must be going through. I have a friend who is raising three autistic children!" He went on to explain that his friend had become a veritable expert on the subject, detailing some of the things she had done to get her kids the help they needed. "I know my friend would want you to give her a call." He then handed me her number and his.

I thought, *How amazing that there was somebody in the room that night who was listening and willing to help me, no less with access*

to a friend who was obviously well informed and willing to discuss it.
I have to say that meeting Rob that night didn't feel like an accident. I later found out that he didn't usually attend that meeting, but he serendipitously showed up on *that* night when I needed him most. It was like God said, "Okay, we're going to throw John a huge life preserver, putting somebody in his path who can guide him." It reminded me of that day at the library two years earlier, just before I entered the program, when I "accidentally" noticed a book and opened it up to the page about AA. It seemed arbitrary, but it wasn't. This was no coincidence either.

I called up Rob's friend the next day. And over the next hour on the phone, with kindness and patience, she cut through our questions with focused, detailed answers, far more helpful than anything the psychologist said. First off, we learned that there was no cure for ASD and no medication to treat it. Nor was there a blood test to screen it.

"It's a subjectively diagnosed disorder," she said. "Even with symptoms such as losing eye contact and the lack of responsiveness, the signs of autism can be subtle and can vary from day to day. It does with my kids. It's never black and white. You have some days when you feel as if you're falling into a black hole with no hope in sight. Your child is unresponsive and just sits alone in a corner, dazed. And then you have other days when your child smiles at you or devours a scoop of ice cream and you feel love rushing into your heart, savoring the moment, doing everything you can to help them connect and feel happy. Hard as it is some days to function, there is always hope. It's like AA, one day at a time." Perhaps she learned this from her mother-in-law, Margaret, who was an icon in AA.

She also talked about possible medications to reduce symptoms, what to expect (it's a slow process), and which doctors and therapists to go see. She was a gold mine of information, leading us to resources that were beyond anything we could have otherwise found. It was almost like she was giving us a master playbook for autism, telling us *who was who* and *where to go*. And even though there weren't that many "plays," with only limited resources at the time, she gave us the wealth of her experience. For treatment, she said, "Although you could either go to a neurologist or a psychologist, neurologists tend to see fewer cases of autism and typically have less interaction with children, whereas a psychologist could make a better behavioral diagnosis."

It would turn out that Gregory was a textbook case for ASD, exhibiting virtually every characteristic, including the avoidance of eye contact, a lack of response to verbal cues (not even noticing when we called his name), and an absence of facial expressions—like happy, sad, angry, surprised. In fact, from the time autism took control of my son at age two, it did so with an iron grip. It was a deep-seated control. Greg wasn't interested in interacting with people, nor did he sing or dance or play around like other kids do. He just seemed remote and wanted to be by himself. As time passed, you could tell that he had no sense of what other people were thinking or feeling. He didn't react to our emotions. As we would learn, autistic children don't read emotions and rarely notice when others are hurt or upset. But with effective intervention, kids can learn critical language, social, and academic skills.

But we were still just trying to connect the dots at this early stage. And on that first day, we wanted Rob's friend to tell us what to do next. She told us about the treatment that had helped her children the most—Applied Behavior Analysis (ABA), which is considered the most common and best therapy for autism. It's a tool that teaches kids virtually everything about human behavior, including speech, the expression of emotion, social skills, motor skills, and self-help rituals (like personal hygiene and toileting). It's based on the idea that if you continually reinforce positive behaviors, the repetition itself will lead kids to repeat those behaviors and lessen problematic acting out like hurting themselves or others.

This turned out to be the best advice we were given, and we will always be grateful to Rob's friend for pointing us in the right direction. In the following days, one conversation with her led to another. And each time, talking with her made us feel a little bit better because it gave us a sense of control, albeit a false sense. But at least we were doing *something*, trying to understand autism and how to deal with it.

We began to encourage Greg to respond and to look at us. But he just wouldn't. I was going to do everything possible to get him the help he needed to maximize whatever he *could* do. We soon consulted with a Norwegian American clinical psychologist named Ivar Lovaas, who had cofounded the Autism Society of America. He was considered a pioneer in Applied Behavior

Analysis, teaching autistic children through prompts, modeling, and positive reinforcement. He showed us some data proving that autistic children could make great progress with what was called Discrete Trial Training (DTT).[1] It's a structured teaching strategy that falls under the umbrella of ABA, designed to help kids with their speech and language skills. It's a technique that breaks down daily life skills into small "discrete" components, using tangible reward reinforcements for desired behaviors.

For example, to get Gregory to look into my face and make eye contact, I used to hold a chocolate M&M between my eyes. That action would capture his complete attention. At first, he was just looking at the candy. And we gave him the reward immediately. But with repetition, we could stretch it out and eventually get a consistent result without any reward given at all. So even when you put the M&Ms away, he *was* making eye contact. But this took years to happen. I would sit one-on-one across the table from him. And together, we would work on one particular task over and over and over again with that reward system in place, whether it was the M&M or a piece of cake.

The next initial goal was getting Gregory to talk or even utter a sound. I would hold up an apple or point to a picture of an apple in a book and repeat "apple" over and over again. It took him forever to say the world *apple*. To teach the color red, we would point to a red apple or a red truck and repeat the word *red* over and over again. Once he said it, we would reward the behavior with a

---

1 Lauren Elder, "What Is Discrete Trial Training?," Autism Speaks, accessed April 2, 2025 https://www.autismspeaks.org/expert-opinion/what-discrete-trial-training.

piece of candy or a small toy. Then we would move on to teaching yellow and ask about both colors. Eventually, after constant drills and rewards, Greg could recognize and name all his colors. It was slow, incredibly tedious work.

Another aspect of the system is setting up a so-called rein-forcement board. For example, if we wanted Gregory to recognize shapes by putting a triangular block into the correct slot, we would model that behavior over and over again, just like the colors. Once he got it right, we would give him a Velcro token star, moving it from one side of the board to the other. After he did three of the exercises correctly, his reward was taking a three-minute break to watch a video, or have some soda, or take a walk. Every time he got an exercise right, it was a small victory for us. And we did this with Greg for years on end. Almost no learning came naturally to him, so *every single thing* had to be taught in this manner. It was daunting and exhausting work, not only for us but certainly for Greg as well.

After hours and hours and hours of repetition, Gregory would eventually understand the *connections* between an object and a function and his own desire to use that object. It was like a light switching on. At one point we felt as if we were going to have to teach him literally every single thing in life that needed to be learned, that he could do no learning on his own. But some windows did open up slowly over time, just not all of them. Some never have.

One time, when Greg was taking a break from the desk where we were working, I turned my back just for a second. And in that moment, Greg snuck a cookie. I got upset and said, "What did you just do?!" His eyes uncharacteristically locked in on mine, and I said, "Did you take a cookie?"

"No." He *lied* to me—and I was ecstatic! Why? Because the behavior was so typical of what any kid would do.

But there were other developmental behaviors that were burdensome. One of the most challenging aspects of raising Greg was the issue of potty training. Even as he reached the age of five, we could not toilet train him. It was an amazingly difficult situation. He would create messes all over the house. He would pull his diaper off when you weren't looking and step in it and track it through the house. A couple of times he painted the basement walls brown. I hate to be so explicit and disgusting, but it was difficult. And I remember that I couldn't get the stench out of my hands for what felt like days. By the time he was turning six, the problem still persisted, so it was not a little baby's poop. Pardon the pun, but this was *serious shit*.

It was a very taxing time, to say the least, because I was also growing my business and actively attending AA meetings at night. Most evenings, after work and helping out around the house, I would leave at 7:00 p.m. to go to a meeting. On more than one occasion, Amy would have to call me on the phone in the car to summon me, saying, "You have to come back. He made a disaster. I need help."

"Autism gave parenting a whole new spin," she says now. "But with or without autism, John and I generally presented a unified front (even if we disagreed with each other, which was rare). We both had a sense of humor about difficult situations, and when one of us would be overwhelmed or unable to deal with a situation, the other just naturally stepped in."

Parenting Greg was a team effort for Amy and me. Without discussing it, Amy and I took turns cleaning up after Gregory, doing what we had to do. There were days when one of us had a little bit more in the tank than the other, so one of us picked up where the other one couldn't. Although we didn't articulate it at that time, we had this natural ability to alternate and share the work. We innately knew when the other partner was at their wit's end and needed a break. Of course, sometimes we would look at each other and just break down and cry. The daily grind creates a pressure inside you. There are times when you feel aggravated, impatient, or incredibly sad. As I read about it later, the parents of children with autism typically worry about everything from lifetime dependency of their child to societal acceptance. Parents of children often experience shame in regard to their child's inappropriate behavior (like meltdowns in public) and that behavior being misunderstood by others. Dealing with all these emotions and pressures eventually motivated us to join parent support groups. The victories were small and far apart.

In terms of Greg's schooling, we wound up hiring a constant flow of private tutors to come. We set up a classroom, a school, in the house. To keep the effort organized, we had a big whiteboard set up in the kitchen with a complete schedule of all the tutors. During the early years, we had to do this because it would have been impossible for him to learn in a preschool environment.

The tutors worked tirelessly with Greg. We had index cards and loose-leaf notebooks divided into sections, itemizing programs and curriculum. It was elaborate. Everything was color-coded for Gregory. Back in 1990, there weren't stock pictures of facial expressions easily accessible, so we took our own photos back then—pictures of people looking surprised or sad or happy or angry. We showed him one card at a time to teach him emotions. But it was very hard because Greg's natural instinct was not to engage at all. He had an aversion to it. In fact, it can be painful and even extraordinarily uncomfortable for an autistic child to look at you. He just could not, would not, and did not want to read your face.

We knew we couldn't possibly handle all this alone. So, during the early years, in addition to private tutors, there were various psychologists and practitioners who were helping teach us how to teach him. First there was Dr. Howard Schneider, the psychologist we worked with after the original diagnosis. But that relationship didn't work out, as Howard had a rather condescending and abrasive personality. As fate would have it, he left the state anyway.

After that, we met a brilliant young fellow named Keith D. Amerson, an expert in ABA who had an amazing gift working with children with autism. He had other talents too. Earlier in life, Keith had been a promising basketball player at Kansas State University, playing two seasons for the Wildcats before finding his true calling working at UCLA's Young Autism Project. He eventually moved to New Rochelle and founded a company with twenty-five employees that served about ninety kids in various school districts. He was the driver of Greg's curriculum, monitoring his progress while supervising staff, who were mostly college students majoring in special education, honing their ABA and discrete trial skills.

Keith was really a genius, an amazing human being, the most gifted educator that we ever met. He understood intuitively what was most important to teach and the *order* in which to teach it. And he always took responsibility for the results: "If the learner isn't learning, it isn't *because* of the learner. It is the teacher's responsibility." That's a very important premise for every aspect of education, but in particular for special education.

When we first met Keith, we explained that Greg was not talking or making eye contact at all, nor did he interact with his sister or other kids. He was a total loner and just didn't want to be a part of what was going on. Keith brilliantly brought our son out of his shell. I have such fond memories of him picking Greg up and lifting him in the air, both of them laughing with joy. Nothing made me happier. When we felt stuck and discouraged as parents by one of Greg's behaviors, Keith was always the man with a plan. He just had this natural gift of engaging with autistic children and getting through to them. His total instinct was to help.

Keith tragically died of cancer at age forty-eight. His impact on Greg, and the autism community as a whole, will never be forgotten.

Slowly, with Keith's help, little by little, Greg developed some limited language. It took years, but eventually he could point to a thing and label it. For example, he'd point to an airplane and know what it was. He'd point to the refrigerator and say, "Drink." That's the thing about autistic kids: They can clearly communicate in short spurts but with no extra expression. And if a kid does point, it's usually because they're trying to get something for themselves—*not* to socially engage you.

Greg would obsessively repeat things that he wanted or comment on environmental things that were happening around him. "It's raining. It's raining. It's raining. It's raining." Over and over again. Yes, we would teach him to make social comments about the weather because that was appropriate. But when he would obsessively repeat things, it was obviously frustrating. Amy and I often felt defeated, but we rarely lost our patience with Greg. We had an expression: *The autism is winning today, but we fight again tomorrow.* Yes, this too, was a challenge to be taken one day at a time. So we had to stay strong.

*   *   *   *   *

During these first years of Greg's diagnosis, Amy and I tried anything and everything we could to find the most effective treatments available. Our goal was to make our son the best he could possibly be. And in our quest to heal Greg, we turned to some treatments that were very controversial.

For example, we flew to California with Greg to meet with some of the renowned ABA experts in the field. In addition to Greg following the ABA therapy that he was already receiving, we also tried chelation therapy. It's a treatment that involves administering chemicals designed to bind to heavy metals (lead, mercury, iron, and arsenic) and eliminate them from the body. (We later learned that chelating agents have a legitimate use in the treatment of poisoning from metals, but there is no evidence that supports chelation as a safe treatment alternative for autism, because autism is not caused by metal poisoning. But we tried it anyway. It did nothing.)

We then turned to a drug called Diflucan, an antifungal that is supposed to rid the gut of yeast, anecdotally reported to have cured or made huge improvements in children with autism. But again, it didn't work, nor is there any evidence to support any antifungal agent as an autism cure.

Next, when Greg was about six years old, we turned to a drug called secretin, a hormone that controls digestion. I was intrigued by reported cases of autistic children greatly improving after receiving the secretin injections. The news of this spread like wildfire throughout the autism community. It was off label for use for autism, and doctors wouldn't write a prescription for it. But I would not accept this. If there was a chance of it working, I wanted to try.

I checked with my doctors and with experts in the field, including a liver specialist who said it was safe. Among the many questions I asked, the last one was the most important: "If he were your son, would you try it?" His response was, "Yes, definitely. But I won't write the script." I then had to figure out how to get the drug, which all our friends in the autism community were also trying to obtain.

I turned to Taryn's brother-in-law, Orlando, a pharmacist who was married to Taryn's sister Elia. Orlando was simply one of the sweetest, most well-intended guys you could ever meet. In the past, we had struck a great rapport and always sought each other out at the large family gatherings. We felt a bond. When I told Orlando about the secretin, he promised he'd look into it. After reading all about it in medical journals on the drug's success, he concluded that the drug was relatively safe. The next day when I went to his pharmacy, he locked the door, showed me the receipt of what he paid for the drug—and I walked out with my first vial of secretin. He simply said, "I just pray it works, John."

There was one immediate challenge: The secretin had to be administered through an IV.

I turned to Taryn and Richie's other brother-in-law, Arthur, a very wise internal medicine MD, and our own personal physician and great friend. In fact, Amy and I were so close to Arthur and his wife, Jayne, that we'd go out to dinner with them all the time, more than any other couple we socialized with in thirty years. As we watched his medical practice grow by leaps and bounds, Arthur watched with the same enthusiasm how we were growing Men on the Move. We became buddies, allies in life, always rooting for each other. (One of their sons was named Greg too.)

Anyway, I approached Arthur and asked him if he would administer the secretin to Greg. He, too, said he'd first have to research it, which he did. Ultimately, he agreed to proceed with the treatment. For the next several months, we would go to Arthur's office on Sunday afternoons when his office was closed. We'd pull the office blinds down and put our little boy on the exam table as Arthur administered the medication. We waited and prayed for several months to see improvement. But again, there was none.[2]

We felt a profound sense of disappointment. In fact, Amy and I were in agony over this for weeks, so discouraged that all three potential medical cures were totally ineffective. The stress of getting our hopes up and then being let down led us to feeling anxious and depressed. So often in the medical world there *are* quick fixes. But for autism, this was not the case. It took months to accept that we would have to be incredibly patient and work with an entire team of practitioners to help Greg in any way we could. We would have to proceed with conventional treatments for his socialization and development in school.

During the first years of tutoring Greg at home, an incredible behaviorist named Toni Ann came into our lives. She had been working with Keith, who valued her highly. Nobody became more important in my son's life and his education than Toni Ann, who came over to our house three hours a day, six days per week. A dark-haired young woman in her twenties, Toni was like a sponge, incredibly talented and really good at understanding behavior modification. Toni bonded with Greg and instantly had instructional control over him. Because he liked her and wanted to please her, he was more responsive to her than anybody else. Their bond would last a lifetime. In fact, at one point, we even made Toni Greg's legal guardian if anything should ever happen

---

2 To this day, the National Institute of Child Health and Human Development states that the efficacy of secretin in ASD treatment is unknown. For us, it didn't work. So we realized that there would be no quick cure.

to Amy and me. (Since that time, Lauren is now old enough to assume that protective role when it becomes necessary.) Toni Ann turned out to be the greatest advocate and ally in my son's life. She truly understood him. As Amy remembers it,

> Toni was a master in behavior analysis. She knew that persons with autism need structure and clear direction, which is actually soothing for them. They have to learn what your *expectation* is for their behavior. And Toni was always consistent and clear with Greg, so there was no confusion as to what she expected— no mixed messages. And because she was so consistent with him, he learned quickly. Toni taught Greg everything from putting sentences together, to saying please, to telling time, to counting money, to crossing the street—everything. She taught Gregory to make his bed, to recognize people, and to identify various rooms of the house (through pictures) so he could follow a direction to "put this in the living room."
>
> Of course, Gregory wasn't always cooperative or compliant. There were times he would throw a tantrum when Toni walked into the house. But she never flinched and always managed to calm him down. Gregory soared with Toni, though she would often attribute his rapid progress to us. For sure, we were an involved family. We participated, we cooperated, we

were responsive, and we all worked together as a team to be consistent.

Before Gregory could even read, Toni would create schedules with pictures (and I would laminate them, following her instructions). Whatever materials Toni needed for Gregory—worksheets, clocks, play money, and so on—I would get the materials to make sure she was fully stocked. (Now you can buy the necessary materials or search for them on the internet, but those resources weren't available in 2000.)

Eventually, Toni also taught Greg to read, which really opened up his world. He didn't have to rely on pictures or our verbal directions anymore. It brought him more independence and made him feel empowered and proud. Once Gregory was a teenager and John taught him how to shave, it was Toni who put the note over the bathroom sink that said, "Shave Monday, Wednesday, Friday, and Saturday." And to this day, that's when Gregory shaves. To remind John and I about what Toni wanted Greg to learn, she would leave us Post-it notes *everywhere*. We would find them in our medicine cabinets, inside our dresser drawers . . . anywhere she knew we would look during our natural daily routine.

No matter what the task, Gregory trusted Toni the most, and still does to this day. He felt safest with her. In short, Toni became *family* to us and still is. In addition to her work with Gregory, she was cognizant of Lauren's feelings too, sensitive to the fact that Gregory was getting so much attention. To make up for that, Toni would take Lauren out for special occasions, like a birthday or a recreational outing to an Islander game. So they became close too.

Concurrently with his home tutoring, at age three Greg started school in Queens at the New York Child Learning Institute, a state-certified nonpublic preschool for children with autism. This school turned out to be very overrated, and it was not helping Gregory at all. Toni felt as if the school's approach was holding Gregory back. She believed he needed to be with typical children in the hopes that Greg would mirror the behaviors of other kids.[3]

When Greg was six, we took him to our local elementary school (Glenwood Landing) in the North Shore School District on Long Island, hoping they might accept him. Lauren was already going to school there and liked it. Having both kids together in the same school could be a great situation, with Lauren there to support her brother. The school's principal, Dr. Ed Melnick, was incredibly sensitive to children with special needs and had created a unique integrated program for both typical kids and those with learning challenges. Dr. Melnick would become a major force in

---

3 Years later, our instinct to do this was validated by the Individuals with Disabilities Education Act, which states that autistic children, and those with other developmental disorders, should be placed in the "least restrictive" setting possible—i.e., into an ordinary classroom. And that's what we had in mind.

Gregory's life and would ultimately lead the way in our quest to give our son the best education we could.

But it was borderline as to whether or not Dr. Melnick would admit him. As Amy remembers it,

> Dr. Melnick asked that we set up an appointment at Gregory's school so that he and his team (teachers, speech therapists, psychologists) could observe Gregory in the classroom. (I was later furious when I learned that the head of the College Point school advised Ed and his team that Gregory was not ready for integration due to his behaviors.) Ed then asked us if he could observe Gregory in a different environment, at the preschool he was attending, where he was supervised by Toni. Under her watch, Dr. Melnick called me and said he had seen a completely different child. "If you want to send Greg to our school, we would love to have him."

Dr. Melnick told us, "I cannot guarantee Greg's success, but I promise I will give him every opportunity to succeed." I'll never forget those words. Dr. Melnick kept his promise and thus began an entirely new chapter in both Greg's life and in ours.

CHAPTER 9

IT TAKES A VILLAGE

People
People who need people
Are the luckiest people in the world

—"PEOPLE," JULE STYNE AND BOB MERRILL (1964)

AMY REMEMBERS Greg's transition to the public school and how it impacted Lauren:

> When our public school agreed to accept Gregory to kindergarten (at age seven), Lauren was in the third grade at the same school. After several months, the principal suggested that it was time we began to increase Gregory's independence and have him walk into the school building on his own. Drop-off was in a circular driveway in the kindergarten wing of the

building. I would drop Lauren and Gregory off there in the morning, and to begin the process, Lauren would walk him to his classroom.

On that very first day, I dropped them off, gave Gregory his backpack, and watched Lauren walk into the building without her brother. She wouldn't even turn her head as I called out, "Lauren, please wait for Gregory." So, back in the car Gregory went, a line of cars behind me waiting for me to move so other children could be dropped off. Gregory's routine would be disrupted for the day and mine too. I was so angry and upset with Lauren. We had prepared for this. Thankfully, I had the day to pull myself together and think about how I would approach Lauren.

That night I said to her, "Lauren, if you don't want to walk your brother to his class, it's okay. You just have to tell me. You can't just leave him hanging there and walk away." Her response was not one I ever anticipated. "Mom, all this talk about Gregory coming to my school, and all I get to do is walk him to his class?" Here I thought she resented him being there and didn't want to have anything to do with him. That moment really gave me a different insight into Lauren's feelings about her brother and helped guide my interactions with her going forward. I would arrange with both their teachers to have Lauren be a larger part of Gregory's day. She read to his class and delivered notes to his teacher so she could check on him and make sure he was okay.

To help Greg assimilate into his new school, we decided he would have an aide with him. An aide helps keep your child focused on what's happening in the classroom by helping them find the right book or page, follow instructions, raise their hand, and so on. The aide would also encourage Greg to play and to interact more in the lunchroom and on the playground with other kids. And not least important, the aide also gave us invaluable information about Greg's daily experiences at school. Over the years, there were many aides, mostly young women, some employed by the school and others hired by us. Typically, they would last one to three years.

But that's getting ahead of the story. At Glenwood, as Amy remembers it,

> The first few months were fine, and then all hell broke loose. Gregory started kicking, biting, throwing tantrums. The aide couldn't control him, and he ended up spending most of his day in a room the size of a closet with the aide.
>
> I went to Dr. Melnick and asked him if we should begin looking for another placement. He sadly shook his head to signal no. "I can't ask Gregory to leave until we've tried everything." Ultimately, I was able to find another aide who knew Greg and had

control over him. Dr. Melnick hired her. And gradually Gregory's acting-out behaviors diminished.
With more consistency and more structure, he made
it through kindergarten and moved on to first grade.
Dr. Melnick very carefully chose Gregory's teacher
each year and allowed us to lead the process of finding
new aides for Gregory as needed. He even initiated a
meeting to have the school district pay for a portion
of Gregory's home program (unprompted—we never
asked). Gregory flourished because Dr. Ed Melnick
provided the supports needed.

John and I would meet biweekly with Dr.
Melnick, Gregory's teacher and therapists, the
aide, and Toni or Keith as consultants. Making sure
Gregory had what he needed and that the staff was
supported was our top priority. We were especially
concerned that Gregory would not interfere with the
learning of the other students and conveyed that to
Dr. Melnick frequently.[1]

During the fifteen years that Greg was a student in the North
Shore school district, Toni Ann was his constant educational
guide and guardian angel. She eventually wound up working for

---

1 Eventually, when Dr. Melnick became the superintendent of the school district, Amy ran
for the school board and stayed on it for the next twelve years—three of them as president. She
worked very closely with Dr. Melnick and formed a deep friendship with him. "He was such
a dynamic leader and cared about every single child," she says. "He was truly one of the best
things that ever happened to North Shore."

the school district, modifying the curriculum dramatically for Greg and kids like him, most notably creating a life skills program under her direction. The program focused on giving kids like Gregory a real-life skills education (reading a menu, telling time, managing money, making and answering a phone call) as opposed to college preparation or prep for the Regents Exams. Gregory's class would make field trips to the supermarket (to learn how to work off a grocery list, put things in a wagon, and pay), make trips to a restaurant to order off a menu and pay, and so on. And throughout this period, Ed Melnick continued his unwavering support, particularly after he became the superintendent of the entire district.

Like many special needs kids who move through a conventional school, Greg remained in the North Shore school district until he was twenty-one years old, making his way through elementary, junior, and senior high school at his own pace. It didn't really matter how quickly he progressed grade-wise. Just being around his peers was very important from a social point of view.

From the beginning of Greg's education, Amy and I were totally involved. I was always part of any decision made and never missed a CSE meeting (Committee on Special Education, consisting of volunteer parent members who advocate for all the autistic and special needs children). I wasn't just physically there. I was totally present. That is one gift of sobriety, giving my children the complete attention they both deserved, something I was not able to receive from my own parents. As time passed, both Amy and I wound up expanding our roles by becoming CSE parent members, which requires a four-hour certification course. It was super rare for fathers to participate. Of the group of seventy members, there were just two dads. All the rest were women! But I wanted to be there for my son and for those other kids. When I walked into a CSE meeting, people would be grateful that I was there to advocate for their child. And since Amy and I had both accumulated a lot of knowledge and experience, we were able to share it, which felt wonderful.

As Greg matured, despite all our efforts, his communication skills remained very limited. He could understand more than what he could put in words. For example, if you say, "Greg, first we're going to go to the dry cleaners, and then we're going to go to the restaurant, and then the movies," he'll take that all in and understand it. But he won't comment on it or ask questions about it. He'll just say, "Yes." He still isn't very expressive to this day. He doesn't talk in complete sentences or in multiple sentences. Everything he says is staccato, so he never or rarely ever tells you really how he feels or what he's thinking. He'll just tell you what he wants, with no social commentary.

We eventually realized he had obsessive-compulsive disorder. When he got out of the car at home, he would have a ritual of first having to walk behind the car and then walk around to the basketball hoop that was in the driveway. If you disrupted that route to the front door, he would throw a mini tantrum. It would be quite a protest. You wouldn't get a full-blown thrashing around on the floor, but he would get upset. You'd have to pick and choose your battles. And you would just let him do some of these less-than-desirable behaviors. To this day, when we drive up to a red light, he has this funny habit of tapping his legs in a certain rhythm as if that's what he needs to do. You let it go because it's not disruptive. We never stopped him because it must, somehow, be comforting for him.

Another thing: When he was younger, he used to be very afraid of the sound of a vacuum cleaner. We broke him of that. How? We introduced the vacuum to him as a friend. We gently told him that the vacuum cleaner was safe and nice and that there was nothing to be afraid of. Eventually he got used to the sound of it, and he could vacuum the carpet on his own.

On the subject of sound, he was also quite bothered by the sound of a baby crying. If we were in a restaurant, even if a crying baby was two hundred feet away from us, Greg was hypersensitive to it. He would start whipping his head around, unable to focus on anything else but that baby crying. But as he grew up and matured, he was able to appropriately tolerate these kinds of sounds. As I said earlier, ours was a world comprised of small victories. With patience, love, and understanding, our son could thrive. That we all believed.

With most of the focus on Greg's behavior and care, it wasn't always easy for his sister, Lauren, to cope with an autistic brother. As acutely as we tried *not* to make our household all about my son, he was getting most of the attention, so Lauren often felt as if *everything* was about him, that her entire childhood was impacted by his condition. Her needs and her desires and her talents and her milestones were often overshadowed by having a brother with constant needs. Friends would come over, and we'd have to keep an eye on Greg to the exclusion of everything else. And, of course, there were many times when Greg embarrassed Lauren badly at a restaurant or out in public. As Amy recalls,

> In 1998, I took Lauren and Gregory to the movies to see *Mighty Joe Young*. It was right after Christmas and Lauren had been given a scarf that she loved and became very attached to. The movie was loud, and Gregory couldn't handle the sensory intake. He started to tantrum. I didn't want Lauren to miss the movie, so I let her stay inside to watch and went into the lobby with Gregory until the movie ended. Lauren would be okay. I stood by the door so I could check on her every now and then.
>
> On the drive home, Lauren realized she had left her scarf in the movie theater and began sobbing, "I hate him, he ruins everything." I was already exhausted from keeping my two kids safe in two different locations and upset from the once again in-my-face reality of Gregory's autism. As I, too, sobbed, my unedited response to Lauren was, "I feel the same way." I dropped Gregory off at the house with John, and Lauren and I retrieved her scarf at the movie theater. It was another opportunity to validate and acknowledge Lauren's feelings and share my own.

Years later, Lauren told us that she felt as if she had to be perfect all the time because there were so many problems with Greg. She just *couldn't* misbehave. And this need to be silent and compliant created a lot of psychological pressure inside her, feeling as if she had to push down her own feelings so that everyone could concentrate on Greg. She had to develop her own coping skills, which is one of the many challenges for a sibling of a special needs child.

Amy spent a great deal of time anguishing over the inequity between the two children. We were keenly aware of the exorbitant amount of attention we had to give to Gregory while being conscious of not giving Lauren enough attention as a result. We tried to balance the intensity of Gregory's needs with the typical parenting of Lauren. And we did the best we could; Amy took mommy-daughter vacations with Lauren annually, but that didn't make up for the everyday losses. Lauren hated that there were always so many people going in and out of the house (therapists six days a week), she was embarrassed by her brother's behaviors in public, and she resented that her brother was different than her friends' siblings.

From my perspective, I did get deep fatherly connection from my daughter. Lauren was a very good athlete, great at both soccer and lacrosse. And during her junior and senior high school days, I wound up becoming the assistant coach of her soccer team, which I loved doing. I've often shared in AA meetings that the happiest times of my adult life were rooting on the sidelines or being in the bleachers, watching my daughter play. She was an absolute joy to watch out there. She was very competitive but also a great team player and a very giving person. She always wanted an assist more than she wanted to make a goal, which is her nature.

I never missed a game for Lauren. That's one benefit of being self-employed—you don't have to ask for permission to take off from work. When you want to leave during the day to attend to your family, you just go. I was very grateful for that. I did everything I could to be a responsible member of the community, not wanting to be like my parents. At one point, Lauren's team competed in the Nassau County championships. I was there in the stands rooting her on at every one of those games. We would drive all the way out to the east end of Long Island, standing forever in the cold, with the wind blowing on the sidelines, freezing our asses off watching these little girls run around playing soccer. I wouldn't have missed it for anything. This was a far cry from what I had experienced from my dad.

As Lauren became a teenager, she became more and more independent. I remember shortly after Lauren got her driver's permit, we went to Jones Beach as a family. Amy and Greg got in the back seat, and I got in on the passenger's side in the front seat. Lauren asked, "What are you doing?" Jones Beach has a very tricky traffic circle around the historic water tower, and when I told Lauren she was driving, she asked, "You're going to make me drive around the big thing in the middle of the circle?" My response was, "Yes!" We made her do that to foster her independence, even though it was a very stressful task for any driver, especially a new one. We threw her right to the wolves, and she succeeded.

Raising two children, one with autism, is never easy, and it creates significant stress on a marriage. In fact, while the divorce rate averages 50 percent for most marriages, it soars to 80 percent for couples dealing with a child with special needs. As Amy remembers it, "It was hard for us to focus on our marriage, manage the business, and take care of ourselves. As much as we made sure to set aside time to go away together, even if overnight, our marriage suffered. I wondered at times if we would survive."

True, the romance went out of the relationship for sure. Our lives were just about hanging on to our sanity, taking care of our children and the business. We weren't making any time for ourselves, because we were totally focused on the kids. We were zombies, consumed with work and parental responsibilities.

To relieve the stress, occasionally, we got someone to stay with the kids overnight. We'd leave the house around 3:00 p.m. on a Saturday and go to a hotel on Long Island (the Huntington Hilton), have dinner, swim in the pool, and go to sleep. We'd get up the next day, have brunch, and be home by 2:00 p.m. We were gone for only about twenty-four hours, but it was still relaxing, a momentary break in the nonstop schedule of being parents and running a growing business.

*   *   *   *   *

We were fortunate that Greg and Lauren got along quite well. Gregory is incredibly passive. He respects and loves his sister, but he is also a little afraid of her. Lauren has a strong personality and

185

communicates forcefully and generally does not take no for an answer. She is very sure of herself. In general, Greg always wanted to please people, perhaps no one more than Lauren. So, when you do make requests of Greg, he's compliant and does what you ask of him. We were also very grateful for that. As he grew into his teen years and then as a young adult, we didn't allow *his* limitations to limit us. We made sure to include him in our lifestyle. We made a conscious decision to not make our world smaller because of him; rather, we made his world larger. We took him into our world, sometimes with more ease than other times, and let him adapt. In restaurants, for example, because autistic kids tend to flap their hands, we had to work on modifying his behavior, teaching him to remain calm and act appropriately.

Greg was never, nor is he now, a natural learner. But we've made him somewhat independent by prioritizing his learning of self-help skills. Our victories included things like toilet hygiene, brushing his teeth, showering, combing his hair (which he is still not great at doing). It took me a year or two to teach him how to shave himself. As many times as I've discussed it with him, he is still not great at it. He doesn't think to change his razor blade, and if there aren't any left, he doesn't think to tell anybody that he needs more.

Greg is now thirty-three years old, an incredibly sweet and good-looking man. Six years ago, we joined with two other families with autistic male adults and set up a house for the three of them to live together. There is a live-in caregiver who looks over the three of them, prepares their meals, and keeps the house running. We did this to make Greg feel and become more independent. It felt like a natural step forward, because Amy and I will not be here forever, and we did not want all the responsibility to fall on Lauren.

Despite these changes, in many ways Greg is still very dependent. He still doesn't have the ability to share what he's thinking or feeling. We understand how his autism has limited his future. He doesn't have the executive function to truly manage his own money. He will never have a relationship or be able to marry. He'll never have children. He'll never drive a car. And as much as I wanted to go to baseball or basketball games with him, he has little interest in doing so. He has more interest in what he is going to eat at the game; he loves the hot dogs and popcorn. He appears to be a very happy and content person. You can tell that he feels productive with his job and loves his routine. Routine is crucial for Greg and for people with autism in general.

*   *   *   *   *

For as long as I can remember, when I thought about being a dad, I imagined having a very close relationship with my son, nothing like the one I had with my own father, who was not present, physically or emotionally. Once I became a father, I was a dad who *wanted* and was *willing* to connect deeply, a dad who was sober and available. I was so looking forward to having a thriving relationship with Gregory, to be present and to speak with him about sports and who won the Knicks or the Yankee game. I wanted to teach him how to drive and how to talk to girls. But none of those things were ever going to happen. Through no fault of his own, Gregory was not available for any of it. He had no desire or ability to communicate with me or anyone else. He just wanted to be left alone.

It felt particularly cruel for both of us. I felt robbed that we would never be able to fully bond in the way I had imagined and hoped for. There would be no deep father-son conversations. The realization of this was very, very painful. It was a huge disappointment, a gut punch that really hurt. I would wonder for years if his condition could have been prevented. I'd tell myself, *Maybe if Amy's doctor hadn't been so rushed on the day of the caesarian, Gregory might have had more oxygen and this wouldn't have happened.* This kind of thinking was crazy, but I was grasping for anything to explain it. There were other times when I read about the evidence supporting the idea that genes are one of the main causes of autism. Then I'd felt guilty about *that*, wondering what was wrong with us. I'd think, *Why was our daughter spared from autism but not our son?* I couldn't fall asleep at times, obsessed as to why in the world this happened to us. But then at other times, I'd think that maybe Gregory's challenge was a gift. In the end, I think I may have become an even more attentive father than I might have been to both my children. I am proud of Greg, and I am proud that he is my son.

While I've described at length my feelings and those of my family, I struggled talking about how Gregory feels. I don't know how Greg feels. I do often find myself imagining what he is thinking and feeling. But I can only wonder. Sometimes I find myself looking at Greg and asking myself, *What is he thinking?* But because I will never know, I look away and process my own feelings.

Amy and I are often asked to describe the experience of raising a child with autism. And we were both moved by a poem we found that captures the essence of some of our experience:

"Welcome to Holland"
By Emily Perl Kingsley

©1987 by Emily Perl Kingsley. All rights reserved.

I am often asked to describe the experience of raising a child with a disability—to try to help people who have not shared that unique experience to understand it, to imagine how it would feel. It's like this . . .

When you're going to have a baby, it's like planning a fabulous vacation trip—to Italy. You buy a bunch of guidebooks and make your wonderful plans. The Colosseum, Michelangelo's David, the gondolas in Venice. You may learn some handy phrases in Italian. It's all very exciting.

After months of eager anticipation, the day finally arrives. You pack your bags and off you go. Several hours later, the plane lands. The stewardess comes in and says, "Welcome to Holland."

"Holland?!" you say. "What do you mean, Holland?

I signed up for Italy! I'm supposed to be in Italy. All my life I've dreamed of going to Italy."

But there's been a change in the flight plan. They've landed in Holland and there you must stay.

The important thing is that they haven't taken you to some horrible, disgusting, filthy place, full of pestilence, famine, and disease. It's just a different place.

So, you must go out and buy a new guidebook. And you must learn a whole new language. And you will meet a whole new group of people you would never have met.

It's just a different place. It's slower paced than Italy, less flashy than Italy. But after you've been there for a while and you catch your breath, you look around, and you begin to notice that Holland has windmills, Holland has tulips, Holland even has Rembrandts.

But everyone you know is busy coming and going from Italy, and they're all bragging about what a wonderful time they had there. And for the rest of your life you will say, "Yes, that's where I was supposed to go. That's what I had planned."

The pain of that will never, ever go away, because the loss of that dream is a very significant loss.

But if you spend your life mourning the fact that you didn't get to Italy, you may never be free to enjoy the very special, the very lovely things about Holland.

*   *   *   *   *

From the moment that Gregory was diagnosed, we went into action—making connections, educating ourselves, and ultimately trailblazing a new path forward through each challenge that we faced. We did a lot of fundraising to support services for those afflicted with autism, to raise autism awareness and to fund research. We consistently attended autism seminars to find out about the latest in therapies and science. We always wanted more information and connections. No matter how much we thought we already knew, we never missed the chance to attend programs, and we always either gained new information or met someone who became part of our growing network. Because we were so deeply involved in Gregory's journey and gained such a breadth of knowledge, we wanted to share our experiences and help other people navigate their own situations. Amy and I received phone calls monthly, sometimes even weekly, from parents who had just received an autism diagnosis for their child, were trying to find an appropriate educational or social program, were working through a child aging out of the school system, or who wanted to set up an independent living situation for their child as we did for Gregory. We never hesitated to help when we were asked. We dropped everything and would take the call. We continue to do so today. Amy has been the lead speaker at several conferences, including one that we hosted for special educators and school officials about how to include children with autism in the general education setting and another that provided information and encouraged parents to explore summer camp opportunities like we did.

As a consequence of the network we built, we became meaningfully involved in several autism advocacy organizations, including becoming founding members of The David Center. Autism diagnoses were growing at a rapid pace, and support services were limited. The David Center was founded in 1999 to provide guidance, education, and support for families of children with autism spectrum disorder. David's mom was a pediatrician and didn't know herself that her son had autism. Her focus was spent on educating other pediatricians and physicians about recognizing autism. The David Center provided support groups, conferences, and much needed access to information.

Shortly thereafter we were introduced to NAAR (National Alliance for Autism Research), a nonprofit research organization founded by parents of children with autism. We helped NAAR grow on Long Island by donating office space to them in our first storage facility. NAAR was eventually subsumed by Autism Speaks, a nonprofit dedicated to creating an inclusive world for all individuals with autism throughout their lifespan. This goal is accomplished through advocacy, services, support, research, and innovation and advances in care for autistic individuals and their families. For many years, we provided office and storage space to Autism Speaks and continue to donate services to assist them with their annual autism walks. Many of our trucks have the Autism Speaks logo painted on them to show our support and to continue raising autism awareness.

In 2005, when Gregory was fourteen years old, Autism Speaks, in conjunction with the David Center, referred us to

a producer at NBC who was searching for a couple to be inter-
viewed for a TV special about raising a child with autism and the
impact that raising a special needs child has on marriage. Initially,
we declined the interview because we didn't want to bring public
attention to ourselves and because we wanted to protect Lauren's
privacy. Also in 2005, while we were of the mindset not to do the
interview, my old haircutter, Vinny, called me and shared that he
had a neighbor who had a child on the spectrum. Vinny shared
with me that the child's father was having a lot of difficulty in
coming to terms with his son's diagnosis and that rather than
really dealing with it, he was just questioning out loud that his
son was "not right." He did not have the bandwidth to admit that
his little boy needed help, and Vinny thought that I could help.
Without hesitation I told Vinny to tell the boy's father to call me.
I waited weeks for that call to come, but it never came.

Amy and I continued our work with Autism Speaks and,
ultimately, we changed our minds and decided to go ahead with
the television interview. Lauren, who was almost sixteen, did not
participate. In the interview, we talked about how the experience
of having an autistic child was different for Amy than it was for
me and how we needed to make time for ourselves and with each
other for our marriage to survive. We did not know at the time of
the interview that the piece would be part of a nationally broad-
casted special, and once it aired, we received supportive calls from
friends and family, far and wide, who had seen our interview.

A few days after the interview aired, Vinny's neighbor, the
mother of the child with autism, called me. She told me all about

her son and how their family was now working to get him more services. She shared with me that she and her husband were watching a special on autism and marriages, and she and her husband were both impacted by this statement made by a father of a child with autism: "I embraced the diagnosis from day one. We met it head-on and it has made a difference." She told me that upon hearing this, her husband broke down sobbing and curled up in a ball. It was a life-changing moment for them. As she was speaking, I knew that she had no idea that those were my words. This interaction was the most direct and personal form of positive reinforcement that Amy and I needed to keep doing what we were doing.

In 2012, we became involved with the Nicholas Center and Spectrum Designs. These two nonprofits were founded in conjunction to provide vocational and paid employment opportunities to adults on the autism spectrum. The Nicholas Center supports the individuals so that they can learn critical life skills, improve social and communication abilities, gain meaningful vocational training, and engage in community projects. Spectrum Designs is a social enterprise that provides vocational and employment opportunities. Spectrum's mission is to create inclusive employment opportunities for people on the autism spectrum.

Other groups that we have supported over the years include Eden II's program, the Genesis School, and NSSA (Nassau Suffolk Services for Autism). These nonprofit organizations offer school-aged programs, adult services, community support, consultation, and transition planning. The Genesis School on Long Island serves students with autism from ages five to twenty-one. Each classroom has a certified teacher and a behavior specialist, a communication specialist, and 1:1 teacher aide as needed. The philosophy of the Genesis School utilizes the principles of Applied Behavior Analysis to provide research-based teaching strategies, which are effective in the education and intervention of individuals with autism. NSSA offers the most advanced treatment and training programs for the benefit of people with autism. Their current associate executive director, who was a parent at the time we got involved with the program, was the first person I reached out to when Gregory was diagnosed. I will forever be grateful to her as her kindness and knowledge base instantaneously put us on the right path.

Each of these organizations continues to provide a wealth of support and information to the autism community.

CHAPTER 10

A MOVING STORY

Ain't nothin' gonna break my stride
Nobody gonna slow me down, oh no
I got to keep on moving

—"BREAK MY STRIDE," MATTHEW WILDER (1983)

I WANT TO take you back to the beginning of my company, Men on the Move. Even before I stopped drinking, Men on the Move was a full-time job. In September 1985, six months before I got into recovery, I took out a business license and placed that first ad in the local *Penny Saver*. My only asset at the time was a 1974 Dodge van with over 200,000 miles on it. But it was enough to get started.

Whenever the phone rang, I would book the job, hop in the Dodge, and do the whole move myself. Simple as that. I was working furiously to build my little business, taking on as many jobs as I could get.

197

Flash ahead a year later: Once I got sober, I was even more focused and determined. Sobriety gave me an obsessive, laser-like focus and an intense sense of responsibility. I would wake up very early for a job that I had probably booked the day before. Even if it was a little job, just moving one or two pieces, I took it. That attitude led to repeat customers, then to referred customers. Instead of going to the bar after a move, I would go back to my home office and check the answering machine.

"Can you move a couch and a chair for me tomorrow?"

I wouldn't wait a minute to call back.

I'd say, "Sure, that's $85 . . . but if you want to do it this afternoon, I could do it for $70. I could be there at three o'clock."

That kind of service works.

Slowly but surely, the jobs started getting bigger. The next year, I bought a fifteen-foot cube truck and plastered the company name across the side of it as big as it would fit. It was good advertising—and a little bit of ego. I wanted people to know we were open for business and could do bigger jobs.

I started moving studio apartments and one-bedroom apartments. Every day I learned something new about the moving business: how to take things apart and put them back together, where to get dollies and blankets (we previously used anything we could find to wrap furniture), how to juggle multiple bookings. The phone kept ringing.

One day I was asked to pick up furniture at a big moving company warehouse. The owner came out to meet me at my truck window.

"Hey, we know you're an unlicensed mover," he said. "I'm letting you go because you're only picking up a few pieces, but you know, you're supposed to get a license."

"I had no idea," I said. "Thanks." I really had no idea.

He could have scolded me or refused me access, even called the state authorities, but he was merciful and kind. I've never forgotten that. He even let me come in and use his bathroom, which is a concern for professional drivers.

In the bathroom I found a copy of *Movers News*, which is the newsletter of the New York State Movers and Warehousemen's Association. I called the association that night, and they told me how to get insurance and a DOT license.

"Amy," I said. "We have to fill out this application and get licensed."

Just like everything else, I plopped it down on her desk and she took care of it.

It took money, but I was making money. As I said, I worked every day and took every job I could book. I would come home after a move, take a shower, and then go visit somebody's house to give them an estimate. At this point, I was renting bigger trucks from Ryder or U-Haul when I needed to.

We took on some employees and got uniforms. My sister Denise's husband, Gordon, created our first logo. To this day, thirty-five years later, we still use elements of the original design. (Our current logo is one of the best-known on Long Island, and for that matter, in the NYC metro moving business overall.)

Over time, I wound up developing a mantra: *Grow by*

one truck a year. My motto was slow and steady growth. In the early days, if I could book enough work and hire enough crew, each truck could yield anywhere between $20,000 and $40,000 annually. Trucks one, two, and three all worked out that way—success on top of success. But after about five years, other business expenses came into play: vacation time, sick days, a pension plan, investment vehicles, and health benefits. It was all necessary if I wanted to keep good people on the payroll. With this kind of overhead, the increased yield per truck decreased as we grew, but we still had to get more trucks in order to make more money.

Amy's cousin Peter came to work for us very early on and has been with us for over thirty-eight years. At the beginning, he was instrumental in working on the trucks. Eventually, as he developed his management skills, he could run crews on his own. When I started focusing more on sales and management details, Peter became the main guy out on the trucks, ensuring that the jobs were being run correctly, maintaining the quality of our work. We always wanted to give people an honest day's work with a sense of conscientiousness and care. Pete was interacting with the clients face-to-face and proved himself to be a great asset to Men on the Move. In terms of his contributions to the business, he was and remains the most successful salesperson in the company's history. He is also without a doubt a very good human being and one of the best fathers that I know.

In the moving business, referrals are key. We got business from everybody—from friends, family, real estate agents, satisfied customers, you name it. One of the greatest sources of business was Amy's maid of honor, Taryn, an original member of The Group. It seemed as if her friends were moving all the time. Referrals galore. Another friend from high school, Janet Sevita, also made tons of referrals. I'm eternally grateful to *everyone* who referred their friends to our moving company. That's how we built the business, one year after another.

I've been asked many times what made Men on the Move so good. First of all, I had a keen sense for connecting with my clients, crawling into their mindsets, and speaking to their needs. I think that was just a natural thing that I may have genetically inherited from my dad.

Second, what separated us from many of the other companies—and I acknowledge, this may sound corny—was purity of heart. We wanted to make a fair dollar for an honest day's work. I put myself in their position and I listened to what they were thinking, what their fears were, what they most wanted from the move. When you empathize and communicate that way, it reverberates with people and it comes back to you as repeat business. I could understand their top concerns: Will your movers take the time needed to wrap everything carefully? Will the furniture and breakables arrive intact? How long will it take to unpack and set everything up?

If somebody asked how much a job would cost, we told them, to the penny, what it would be. There were no extra or hidden charges. To this day, we have a 72.6 percent repeat and referral rate. That means every time the phone rings, over 72 percent of the time it's either a repeat customer or a referred one.

That's powerful, and it speaks to the quality of our systems.

Most importantly, our employees are well trained, friendly, and service-oriented. Our trucks are always clean and well equipped. Each truck has the appropriate number of blankets and dollies (depending on its size). The wardrobe boxes are always in good condition. We never leave garbage in the truck. In other words, we are fastidiously prepared. All this comes down to being conscientious and doing the next right thing.

All the attention to detail paid off. Every year, we got another truck. It didn't make us rich, but, as described earlier, it allowed Amy and I to buy our first tiny house. Then, in 1993, when I was thirty-three years old, our hard work and success allowed us to buy our second home—a cookie-cutter colonial set on a quarter- acre in Glen Head, New York, priced at $413,000. That was a serious amount of money for a house in 1993. We would live there for the next twenty-eight years. We raised our family there; we became active members in the community and made lifelong friends.

When I first started making more in excess of our expenses, I reminisced about a former drinking buddy from the Midland named Cliff, a good friend of my dad and mine. He was a wealthy guy, retired from the day I met him.

"John," he once said to me, "you will never see me driving a car more than three years old." Cliff always drove a new Cadillac.

Cliff's standard stuck in my brain. Once we had the means, I adopted it for myself. I would never own a car more than three years old. Not bad for a recovering drunk who grew up on food stamps. In my early days, I just wanted to catch up to my friends by buying a house and driving a nice car, giving myself material rewards. It was all about my ego kicking in: "Hey, look at me." But as time passed, with years of going to AA meetings and sobriety, I replaced my materialistic focus with a sense of gratitude for the blessings in my life. For someone like me who came from a home with intense alcoholism, an absentee father, food stamps, eviction notices, and nonpayment of rent—experiencing this kind of financial stability was a true gift. And I began to see it and appreciate it more and more.

I was traumatized by what happened to me as a child. That early history unquestionably impacted my hunger for success. I think of it almost as a rubber band or a slingshot effect: The pain and failure were counterbalanced by the pleasure of success and achievement. I never forgot putting those baseball cards on the bottom of my sneakers to keep out the rainwater. By the mid-1990s, I felt gratitude knowing that I could take care of my family and make them feel safe and secure in all the ways that I was not as a child.

By this time, I was sober for at least six or seven years, and the transformation of my life could not have been more dramatic. Amy and I now lived an upper-middle-class lifestyle on the North Shore of Long Island. It was fine. It was comfortable. But I knew that I could accomplish more, and I wanted more for our family.

*   *   *   *   *

My original goal to buy one new truck a year continued, but I looked for ways to expand our business, including attending seminars on the exploding self-storage business. I realized that self-storage and buying and selling warehouses, rather than just moving people, was a much more profitable direction to go in. Around the same time, my sister Denise, who was between jobs, came to work for Men on the Move. Denise stayed with Men on the Move for over twenty years. Her contributions to me personally, and professionally to the company, were integral to our growth and success.

In 1996, I took a leap and signed a lease on a 20,000-square-foot warehouse in Floral Park, New York. The warehouse was 80 percent empty when I leased it; my plan was to fill it with paying customers and more than pay the rent.

This was not self-storage where each customer gets their own lock and key. This was traditional warehouse storage: People give you their things. You wrap them up, tag and inventory them, and keep them in the warehouse under your care, custody, and control. When the owner needs them back or wants them shipped, you give them back or ship them. At this point, Amy and I were running Men on the Move, the moving company, plus, of course, raising Lauren and Gregory . . . so we had our hands full, and we didn't have extra money to lose on the new warehouse business, but I did not see it as a risk. It was a good bet, a natural extension of the moving business.

The leased warehouse was part of a big complex at 50 Carnation Avenue in Floral Park. The landlord's name was Kermit

Gordon. He was a tiny little guy with green eyes, and he always wore French cuff shirts with beautiful emerald cuff links. Green eyes, green cuff links, that was his thing. Kermit was a classy, terrific guy, and we liked each other a lot. Based on that relationship, we negotiated a deal that would ultimately change my life: I would get rights of first refusal to any other space in the complex if it became available to rent.

Eighteen months after making my deal with Kermit, he called me up to tell me that a 35,000-square-foot space had become available in the complex. Coincidentally, I had just recently attended another seminar on self-storage where I learned about the process of doubling the floor space of a high-ceilinged warehouse by turning one floor into two. This possibility was on my mind when Kermit walked me around the newly available space. It had high ceilings.

Kermit and I negotiated the lease of a lifetime: I signed a twenty-year lease with a ten-year term at $6 a foot. And because of the ceilings, I could double the square footage at my own expense by installing a second floor, lowering the cost per square foot to about $4 all in. That's incredibly cheap. The only problem was that I had to pony up the cash for the build-out myself. Was I really going to build a self-storage facility from scratch after attending just a couple of self-storage seminars? It was a crazy idea.

To this day, I have trouble reconstructing where we found the money—over $1 million needed for the construction. Amy and I pulled out all the equity from our house; we begged, borrowed, and stole from anybody we could; we borrowed money against a life insurance policy; and we worked like maniacs, draining every dollar out of the moving business. It would have been comical if it hadn't been so risky.

My sister Denise was working with us very closely to support this new venture. She did a financial pro forma and assisted us in getting estimates from contractors while also overseeing the construction. For example, we got estimates for the sprinkler system that ranged from $50,000 to $220,000. Frankly, we were laughing out loud, not knowing what price point was appropriate. Though we had good gut instincts, we really didn't know what we were doing, so we chose a price in the middle. We obviously had never done any of this before, but we were learning all about construction.

The project required dealing with multiple contractors and countless builders, and many permits later, the build-out in Floral Park was complete. We opened what was our first self-storage facility on October 13, 2000. Four months later, on February 4, 2001, we celebrated my fortieth birthday in the new warehouse. Amy planned it as a surprise party, but I knew it was happening. That day, as I arrived at the warehouse, I turned the corner on the loading dock and sixty or seventy of the most precious people in my life were waiting to surprise me, including my sisters, my kids, The Group, and all the friends who had supported me through the years. Having them with me was one of the best feelings in the world. It was the grand opening not just for the new warehouse but a new era for Men on the Move.

I can tell you that we filled up that space fast. It brought in a ton of money, and there was no sign that the money would stop as long as we had our great lease. That lease with Kermit and the build-out of the self-storage facility was both the best and the riskiest financial move that we ever made, as it became the financial backbone and strength of Men on the Move and propelled us forward for all our future successes.

Suddenly our life became financially easier and more comfortable. We were living a really nice life. Reminiscent of the night of my first AA anniversary, I felt as if I could *do* and *have* and *be* whatever I wanted. It wasn't just a feeling; now it was a reality. The business model of buying self-storage warehouses was far more profitable (and less of a daily grind) than taking one moving job at a time. I felt healthier, happier, and more relaxed all around. At age forty, I was now experiencing one of the twelve promises of AA: Fear of economic insecurity will leave you.

That said, I needed to pay back a lot of money for the purchase of that warehouse—hundreds of thousands of dollars to attorneys, friends, banks, and the life insurance company . . . everyone who had helped us finance the construction. We had borrowed a lot to get the space up and running, and now it was time for the believers to recoup. Everyone was paid back, and that felt good.

I was in my mid-forties, business was good, our marriage was surviving the challenges that came with raising a special needs child, a preteen girl, and all the other day-to-day stressors. Lauren was fun and showed signs of being a good athlete, and

Greg was doing okay. Everything really seemed okay until I got a call from Richie, a friend from my LeFrak days.

Richie and I had drifted a bit. I did the migration from Queens to Long Island and already had two kids. Richie married a wonderful girl, Jennifer, in his late forties, and the two of them were still living in Queens. They were struggling to have a child for quite a while. Eventually it happened for them, and they had a beautiful boy named Ross. Well, as one might predict, shortly thereafter Jennifer got pregnant for a second time, quickly and easily. Rich was going to be a dad again. Life seemed good for Richie as well.

But when he called that afternoon, I knew something was wrong just by the tone of his voice. We went to lunch at Bryant and Cooper's Steakhouse where Richie told me that the doctors suspected that he had ALS (amyotrophic lateral sclerosis). It is one of the most debilitating, cruelest diseases there are. That day I watched Richie struggle to cut his steak, he was hoping it was something else. It was ALS, and it took hold of Richie right away. What was *really* difficult for everyone to wrap their heads around was not only that they had a newborn at home but that Jennifer was pregnant again. The weight of that, along with knowing what would be inevitable, was overwhelming. To this day we are all astounded by the grace, dignity, and calm that both Richie and Jennifer demonstrated during this upheaval of their lives.

The LeFrak crew rallied around Richie and Jennifer. No one could have imagined how we all rose to the occasion to try and help. Some of us took him to doctors, some of us planned in detail a special wheelchair, others took care of the boys, and sometimes one or more of us simply spent hours with Richie. On one such occasion, Rich and I spoke about our bucket lists. He wanted to go to the Kentucky Derby. I said, "I'll book it!" But we did not have time to make it happen.

We all did what we could.

The second baby came. It was another beautiful boy. His name is Andrew.

I remember vividly visiting Richie in their Whitestone apartment. We were watching the Yankee game. The announcer focused on Monument Park and mentioned Lou Gehrig and ALS, which is known as Lou Gehrig's Disease. At this point, Rich could hardly move. He was unable to use his hands or raise his arms. He was lying in bed and Jennifer placed both boys, who were still infants, on the bed with Richie. The boys were in diapers, crawling all over him and he was unable to hug them. His eyes, still able to move, looked me straight in the eye, and I watched as tears flowed from his eyes down his cheeks. It's an image that I will never forget the rest of my life.

Even after Richie passed, we all stayed the course. We were all there, and continue to be there, for those boys. Through my involvement which Richie's sons, I fully understand the meaning of "it takes a village," as all of Richie's friends pitched in one way or another to help Jennifer raise the boys. She has done an incredible job.

Today Ross and Andrew are amazing young men doing great in college, and both of them have quite a future ahead of them. I see and speak to them often. They have worked at Men on the Move over the summer and during breaks.

One day, I hope they will come to understand what a good human being their dad—the dad they never knew—was and why his friends cared so much.

* * * * *

The period of 2000 to 2006 was a time of growth for Men on the Move. The business generated significant profits, and I was ready to do more. With the capital and momentum behind us, we found an existing 80,000-square-foot self-storage facility in Huntington, Long Island. I wanted to buy it. I got a good deal on it because I knew the owner, Bill, from the times our company had moved him and his wife. Anyway, Bill was a Renaissance man—an airplane pilot, a very successful car dealer, and a real estate developer who had turned one of his old car dealerships into this self-storage facility. By the time I negotiated with Bill, he was an older man who was getting tired of working. He had lost focus and wasn't maximizing the potential of the property. So, he sold it to me for a good price— $4,250,000—just to get out from under it. I knew I could really turn it around. We had gone from just leasing a 20,000-square-foot warehouse to adding an additional 70,000-square-foot in Floral Park to now adding an 80,000-square-foot self-storage facility in Huntington Park, yielding a total of 170,000 square feet on Long Island. That's what was accomplished by 2006.

Always incremental but always progressing. Just like one truck per year.

Around 2008, after I owned the 80,000-foot place in Huntington for a couple of years, I decided it might be time to expand it. As I considered expanding a space that large, I wanted to consult with a reputable company. I found a local construction company, Racanelli Construction, that specialized in self-storage projects.

At the same time, I continued scouring the streets for other buildings that I could potentially turn into self-storage facilities. I had honed what I call my *spidey* sense, the ability to identify properties that were going to work, just like Spider Man's sixth sense that allowed him to anticipate things. One day, I followed my nose to an old manufacturing warehouse in Glen Cove, Long Island, a tired white stucco building with light blue trim. It stood a little bit higher than the surrounding properties, so it didn't have the ground pollution that these other properties were subject to. I thought this building itself would be perfect to convert from a manufacturing warehouse to self-storage. Anyway, with a little quiet digging, I caught wind that the tenant might be moving out, so I decided to take a chance. I put on a suit, pulled up in a nice car, and walked in as if I owned the place.

"Can I help you?" someone said.

"No, thank you," I said. "I'm just with the insurance company."

Nobody said another word. They let me walk around. I checked out the ceiling height, the columns, the sprinkler system, everything. By the time I left, I knew I wanted to buy that building.

The owner, Larry, who was not a nice guy, and a real piece of work, had lost his tenant and was on the fast track to bankruptcy. We came to agree on the purchase price of $3.5 million for the property. We were really close to signing the contract, in late 2008, when the subprime mortgage mess hit, the stock market crashed, and I had to pull the deal.

"I'm not signing," I said. "The world just changed. The economy is collapsing."

Larry was incensed and called me every name in the book. Admittedly, growing up in gin mills, I'd been around the block, but he used foul language that day that I'd never heard before. My favorite of the AA promises is that *we will intuitively know how to handle situations that once baffled us*. Whenever I'm confronted with something challenging, I pause. I take a deep breath. I think about it. And I then *respond* instead of *reacting*. This practice has made a huge difference in every aspect of my life, whether it's with my children, my wife, my sisters, employees, colleagues, clients . . . or disgruntled business contacts. So even though Larry unloaded on me and called me every foul name in the book, I didn't react; I knew to let it go.

Still, I could *not* let go of the property, which was very close to my house. It became an obsession. Amy laughed at me when I rerouted the car to drive past it. For example, on my way to taking Greg to McDonald's, I would go two blocks out of the way just to drive past the property. I was always scouting the property, wanting to see if anything was going on in there. I would think to myself, *This building has great visibility. This is a densely populated area. This place is a slam dunk.*

Almost three years later, the Glen Cove property fell into bankruptcy, and I purchased the building for $3,125,000—hundreds of thousands of dollars less than it otherwise would have been. But this project was not going to be as simple as the one in Huntington. For starters, the building was in an incredible state of disrepair. One day, I walked through to find rain literally pouring through the ceiling—not like a water hose, but like a fire hydrant. As we moved through the building, we were getting soaking wet. The building needed complete gut renovation.

I was still working with Racanelli Construction on the Huntington expansion project, so at one of our meetings I asked Marty Racanelli if he had ever gone in as partners on a self-storage property. Yes, he had.

"Boy, do I have a property for you," I said.

We formed a partnership with a third party, an accountant named Ben, who Marty had introduced me to. We were equal partners. It was a marriage made in heaven. My sister Denise was always urging me to take on partners. It took a long time for me to come around because I always wanted to be in control of everything myself. I liked being the decision-maker and not having to consult with anyone else. I like executing my own vision without any obstacle or pushback. Yet I finally did take her suggestion. And it's a good thing I did. It was a huge project. And I would have been in way over my head if I had tried to do it by myself. This was just one of the many ways in which Denise has encouraged me throughout my life to expand my thinking. And I'm grateful for that.

While we were involved in the renovation and overhaul of Glen Cove, I continued to search for other properties. I soon found a troubled storage facility in Islandia, Long Island. It was being run by a very nice man who had inherited it and just didn't know the business. Coincidentally, by the time I reached out to him, he had already heard of me and Men on the Move, having read an article in the local paper about my philanthropic work related to having a son with special needs. He told me that he liked what I was doing and seemed very open to discussing a deal. I made him an offer, but somebody else offered him more. You win some, you lose some.

A few weeks later, however, the man called me back. His deal had fallen through, so he agreed to my original offer. It was a great price, but it was a third-class or C facility that needed a ton of work. The Racanellis, Ben, and I bought the Islandia facility for $4.2 million. We then put another $1.3 million into it. Our standards were high, and our collective expertise was hard to beat. We were all equal owners; I served as the managing partner for the shared properties, and Men on the Move was paid a management fee for running the businesses. I was calling the shots and bringing in more money than I, or my partners, ever thought possible. I learned something very important in our experience of purchasing the Floral Park, Huntington, and Islandia properties: In each of those cases, I made a human connection to the seller, which proved to be critical in each of those transactions.

Without solicitation, I started receiving offers on the portfolio of properties owned by us. In part that was because the self-storage business was one of the few industries unscathed by the subprime mortgage crisis, so while the economy was crashing, the self-storage industry remained incredibly strong. This was a profound wake-up call by Wall Street in recognizing self-storage as a great stable real estate asset. Shortly thereafter, institutional investors started throwing money at businesses like ours. One of those investors approached us in 2013. They wanted to buy the self-storage facility in Glen Cove, the property in Huntington (which I owned myself), and the one in Islandia too.

They offered us tremendous money: $35 million for all three! And I got the price up to over $38 million. I was ecstatic. After a little discussion with my partners, we decided to take it. Overnight, my wealth had expanded exponentially. Even though I was already a millionaire, now I *felt* like one. I had come a long way from the days of owning my '74 Dodge. I was still moving and about to go even further.

Around the same time, I was still renting the Floral Park complex, which I had been dying to own for years. Kermit had passed away, and I took that as an opportunity to contact the new owner about a purchase. I was selling my three storage properties and coming into unimaginable money. The new owner asked me to dinner and said, "Let's talk."

I was thrilled and told Amy, "They must want to sell!" Amy was thrilled by this too.

We had been renting this complex on my original terms with Kermit for almost twenty years. No one had ever asked us to go to dinner. Sometimes the stars align. For sure, timing is crucial in both real estate and in life—and serendipity can never be planned for. That night we had a nice meal, and toward the end of it the owner said, "John, it's time for us to talk about selling the whole Floral Park property, if you're interested."

It was now the winter of 2014. If he had asked me a year earlier, I wouldn't have had anywhere near enough money. Now, for the first time ever, I had more than enough. The building into which I had poured all my finances (and a lot of other people's) to refit for self-storage, the building that had formed the backbone of Men on the Move, could finally be mine. We negotiated over a few weeks. Denise and I strategized together on how to negotiate with the seller. We signed a contract and closed quickly at what I believed to be a really good price.

I decided to add a second level to a portion of the Floral Park building and eventually got a permit to make it all self-storage. I worked for over a year and spent over a hundred thousand dollars developing the property. There was money going out to lawyers, architects, civil engineers, you name it. *Real estate development is an exercise in perseverance.* Dot that *i* and cross that *t* . . . executing deals like this is not easy. When I see skyscrapers go up in Manhattan for $2 billion, I am absolutely in awe, even stunned, trying to imagine what really goes into a mammoth project like that. In my world, refitting a 100,000-square-foot facility for self-storage was tough enough, but we did it.

A Moving Story

The Floral Park Station on the Long Island Railroad was directly across the street from my new complex, which made it what they call a TOD zone (transit-oriented development zone). Because it was right by the line, the land was becoming more and more valuable for people who commute into the city. Soon after we completed the overhaul, investors came courting who wanted to buy the building, change the zoning, and make it into an apartment complex.

Between the sale and the development, I invested millions of dollars in the property. Now someone was offering me double my money in what felt like overnight. It felt good to be the sole owner in a position to make that kind of deal.

I seriously considered the offer, but I repeatedly hit the calculator and did some long-term projections—and I figured that the property could be worth a lot more than the offer if it were fully developed as self-storage. In addition, I had trouble wrapping my head around the idea of selling a property that I had wanted for so long and finally owned. I said, "Thanks, but no thanks." My sister Denise thought I was nuts. But Amy trusted my intuition, always deferring to me to steer the ship.

It turned out to be the right move. As soon as the self-storage permit came through, several companies approached me about buying the complex. The bidding started at millions over the first offer. One of the companies that came knocking was a nationally recognized self-storage chain that happened to be the same company that had bought the facilities in Glen Cove, Islandia, and Huntington. When they saw the work that I had done and

217

the permit in my hand, we agreed on a sale price that was three times what I paid for the Floral Park property. I had owned the Floral Park location for only eighteen months, but I had bought it, transformed it, and tripled my money. The timing of all this had been perfect. I felt as if the circle was complete. Now it was time to move out of the space that I had occupied for over twenty years and move on.

After the sale, Amy and I considered retiring. I was fifty-seven at the time. I was always a curious learner and actively investigated the best ways to maximize and use the profits that were the result of our hard work. One of the things that I learned about was called a 1031 exchange, which encourages investors to reinvest their profits in new investment properties. There are a lot of rules to follow for the new investment to be qualified under the 1031 rules. So Amy and I decided if I could find properties that would make the 1031 work, we would do it again.

*   *   *   *   *

From my first real estate grand slams described above, there were several others that followed, some even greater in scope and profit. As my company expanded from a one-man operation to a fleet of twenty-seven trucks, and with my sobriety now in its third and fourth decades, I did feel a sense of true satisfaction. Supporting me through all of it was Amy, who was always indispensable to our success.

CHAPTER 11

CHECKING THE RIGHT BOX

You're not just any girl
No, not any girl, so I knew, I knew

—"Not Just Any Girl," John Beyer (2018)

As EXCITING AS our professional success was, it was our family that always provided the greatest joy.

The date was October 13, 2018.

It was going to be quite the wedding for my daughter, Lauren, and her husband-to-be, Patrick Bardsley. The story of how they met makes me a believer in the power of destiny.

Starting at age eleven, Greg attended a special needs camp called Camp Huntington, located in High Falls, New York, just minutes from Woodstock. It was a fantastic place with five hundred campers ranging in age from seven to sixteen. Greg just loved going there. And it was during his first summer that he met a camp counselor who would change our family forever.

It all started back in the small village of Guilsfield in Wales. There, a sixteen-year-old boy named Patrick Bardsley eagerly applied to Camp America, a program that offered cultural exchange summer jobs for young adults wanting to work in the US. On the application to become a camp counselor, there was one question about whether the applicant was willing to work with special needs kids (defined as those who had chronic illnesses, physical impairments, or cognitive or psychiatric issues). As Patrick was filling out the application, he asked his dad if he should check the box for special needs, indicating a willingness to work with such children. His dad said, "Sure, why not?" believing it might increase Patrick's chances of being accepted into the program. And it was true. Any male who checked that box got scooped up right away. And so it was. As the camp would discover, Patrick was a great candidate. He had a winning demeanor: He was kind, confident, and fun-loving, truly ideal for the job. He was also a very good-looking young man—over six feet tall, athletic, with piercing blue eyes and fine features. It didn't hurt that he had a classic British accent and spoke the Queen's English. He was a natural leader and a great communicator. No doubt, he would be a great addition to the staff. Based on his referrals and enthusiasm to make the commitment, he got the job and started to work at the camp in June of 2006.

That first visit to the US was just the beginning of Patrick's American adventure. He was gifted and bonded easily with the kids. Without any training as a bunk counselor, he immediately met their needs with sensitivity and patience. He seemed to have an intuitive understanding of how to interact with them, each child having a different personality and unique needs. More than he even expected, Patrick found working with this population of kids immensely rewarding. In fact, he liked it so much that he came back summer after summer for five years straight.

Each summer, Amy and I would drop Greg off and then check in with this young guy from Wales to see how Greg was adjusting to the camp life. Amy would send Patrick periodic text messages to see how Greg was doing, in addition to making a weekly phone call. Patrick was always pleasant, conscientious, and caring of our son. We really appreciated his sensitivity and genuine interest in Greg's welfare. And because of our frequent check-ins, we developed a really nice rapport with him. Amy remembers that period:

> Every summer we would send Gregory to camp with a photo album of our family so he could share it with his counselors. Patrick seemed to take an interest in Lauren. On one Sunday, I had asked Patrick to please have Gregory call Lauren, as she felt left out not hearing from him. Patrick had a cell phone that he used only in the States and entered Lauren's number into it. And that was the end of it, but not in my mind.

221

All through Greg's years at Camp America, I secretly thought Lauren and Patrick would make a cute couple. But it was totally impractical: At the time, Lauren was sixteen and Patrick was eighteen. She lived in the States, he in Wales. How silly! Yet he had seen her picture and apparently liked it, which I would find out later. Meanwhile, I encouraged Lauren to look Patrick up on MySpace (the precursor to Facebook).

When Amy and I went to the camp on family weekend visitations, Lauren never made the trip with us and therefore never actually met Patrick. But every time we'd come back home, Amy would say, "Lauren, you *have* to meet this guy Patrick, Greg's counselor. He's soooo good-looking." I'd just roll my eyes.

When we picked Gregory up on the last day of camp in his fifth year with Patrick, Patrick told us that he had just graduated university and would be coming to the States to live in Manhasset, just a few towns over from us. He had found a family willing to sponsor him. (We actually knew the family, as Gregory had bunked at the camp with one of the boys.) As Patrick explained to us, with a student visa, he could both study in the US and work here too. He announced that he would be studying for his master's in special education with a concentration in autism. As he proudly told me, "Mr. Beyer, I'll be attending a university on Long Island. Perhaps you've heard of it. It's the C. W. Post campus of Long Island University."

"Do you know it?" he asked.

"Patrick," I replied, "I could walk there from my house!" I felt this was a good thing since Greg liked him and could possibly spend some time with him.

One night, during Patrick's freshman year at C. W. Post, Lauren and Gregory were at a local pub getting hamburgers for dinner. Patrick happened to be there, at the bar, having a pint with some of his classmates. Gregory got up and crossed the room to go to the bathroom. Patrick saw him and then glanced back at the booth and figured it must be *her*. Patrick—who remembered he had Lauren's cell phone number in his American phone from years before—immediately walked over to Lauren and said, "*You* must be Lauren Beyer." He had been hearing about Lauren for years and seeing her photos in Gregory's scrapbooks, including one of her in a white Ralph Lauren bikini, which was obviously memorable. Lauren looked up, startled by Patrick's good looks, and replied, "From that accent, *you* must be Patrick Bardsley." At last, the introduction was made.

The rest, as they say, is history. As Amy puts it, "Patrick checking that box on his camp application brought him into Gregory's life, charted his professional career, and paved the way to his marriage." Yes, this accidental introduction changed everything. Almost right away, Patrick and Lauren started dating and gradually fell in love. At the beginning, of course, they naturally discussed Greg and autism, his schooling, and Patrick's camp experience.

"While they were dating," says Amy, "Patrick shared with

me that Lauren had told him, 'Even if we don't make it, you have taught me so much about my brother.' Patrick's patience, understanding, and interactions with Gregory have been invaluable to our family. No longer did Lauren have to explain or feel embarrassed about Gregory now that she was with Patrick. She was safe."

Beyond talking about Greg, Patrick and Lauren quickly discovered that they both loved and played soccer, a definite bond. In fact, on their first "date," Patrick came over to our house to pick up Lauren, grab a soccer ball, and then head over to the school field to kick the ball around. They were both excellent athletes and competitors. Although Lauren liked Patrick, she played very hard to get, often ignoring Patrick's requests to go out. In fact, she famously remained reticent in response to his invitation to bring her to an event on the floor of the New York Stock Exchange. He texted her for days, but she didn't respond. Eventually, she did go to the Stock Exchange event with him, and after that they began seeing each other regularly.

Early on, Patrick gave her a laminating machine (for her flower-pressing business) as a birthday gift. Yes, roll your eyes. I thought that it might be a deal-breaker, but they withstood that incredibly unromantic gesture. We all laugh about it today. As time passed, they certainly had some rocky moments, as everyone does in any relationship. But year after year they stayed together. The relationship had become a very serious and real one. And while it was obvious to all that a proposal seemed imminent, Patrick would not *would not* propose until he had a green card, lest anyone ever think that the marriage was one of convenience.

Well, after a four-year courtship, and after finally obtaining a green card, Patrick very intentionally and nostalgically asked Lauren to marry him back at that very same pub where he first met her. It was also at the pub, a week earlier, that Patrick asked for our blessings to marry Lauren. My reaction was memorable. I went into the full father-protector mode. Though I wasn't surprised by his proposal, I did find myself asking him a lot of questions: "When you fight, do your guts get twisted? Do you realize that *love* is a verb? Are you sure this is what you want?" I unwittingly was giving him a very hard time, almost interviewing him. Yet, on the inside, I think I was quietly very happy. I just wanted to be sure he was sure. Lauren and Patrick mock me about this today. Patrick will say, "You gave me a very hard time!" Patrick made sure that Greg was there as well. It seemed very fitting since Greg, while not formally, is really the one who introduced Lauren to her husband.

As for the wedding plans, Lauren wasn't the big wedding type, so she wanted to keep it small and humble. While Lauren has many, many friends, she tends to be demure and more low-key. But Patrick and Amy wanted something grander, a large celebration with lots of friends and family present. Patrick also has nine siblings, many friends, and family, so over sixty people from Wales made the trip across the pond to be at this celebration.

225

While the size of the wedding party may have been a point of contention, there was one definite thing that both Patrick and Lauren agreed on: They both wanted a wedding venue with a view. And boy, did they get one, renting out the Grand Hall on Ellis Island. The ceremony was held outside, facing a spectacular view of Lower Manhattan and the Statue of Liberty. Along with the view came the three hundred guests!

On that late afternoon in October, the reception was spectacular. We were blessed with a bright blue sky above the backdrop of Lower Manhattan. We had the American flag along with the Union Jack hanging in the Great Hall where all the immigrants had at one time passed when first coming to America. Lauren looked so beautiful in her white gown, and I felt incredibly proud of her. The father-daughter dance went perfectly. All in all, I have to say that Lauren got the song and the view, while Amy and Patrick got the big wedding.

When you think about it, the series of circumstances (and coincidences) that had to occur for this wedding to take place were pretty amazing. Greg had to go to that summer camp. Patrick had to want a job in the US. The bond between Greg and Patrick had to grow. And then one day Lauren had to be sitting at the pub for the introduction. The rest was history. It's amazing how sometimes "the stars align," which is one of the lines in the wedding song I'd written for Lauren.

*   *   *   *   *

About six months prior to Lauren getting married, my never-ending love for music inspired me to take piano lessons. I had never before played any musical instrument. But as I wrote earlier, I had done some singing at school. And when my mother asked me to sing Andy Williams and Frank Sinatra songs for her, I loved doing it, as it gave me much-needed attention. And on my own, with just the radio, I found listening to music offered solace and solitude, especially during my childhood, when I needed comforting the most. So here I was, decades later, taking piano lessons. Over the years, I have also been asked to sing at several weddings we've attended.

Although the piano was the only instrument I ever imagined playing, it took only about two dozen lessons for me to realize that I was never going to be a great pianist. I just wasn't a natural at it. But in the midst of this musical experiment, something interesting happened. While planning Lauren's wedding, we were trying to choose a song for the traditional father-daughter dance. Lauren and I both love music and have the same taste: I got her hooked on the Beatles and seventies pop music, and we felt a real connection to it as a shared experience. We were nonetheless having trouble choosing the right song for that important father-daughter dance. It drove me nuts. But one day at the keyboard, using just one finger, I started tapping out a melody. The hook and my own song lyrics just came to me. I filled it in with some chords and finished it quickly. The song is called "Not Just Any," and the lyrics go like this:

Live a Little Better

My dear daughter
Allow me to tell you
How I feel
No one has written the words
No one has written the song
That tells you how your father feels . . .

You're not just any girl
No, not any girl
So I knew
I knew
It couldn't be just any boy
Not just any boy
For you

You have that smile
That warm inviting heart
So full of love
Your daddy's little girl
Always my little girl

No, not just any boy
Not just any boy
I wouldn't have it
I wouldn't have it
No, not just any boy
Not just any boy

CHECKING THE RIGHT BOX

For you

I worried for no reason
Your mom had done the job
You're the one he'd have to fear
You're the one he would endear

Sometimes the stars align
No, you're not just any girl
He's not any boy
No, not any boy
No, not any boy
No, not any boy
For you . . .

After finishing up the song, I recorded it in a local studio so it could be played at the wedding for our dance—I knew I didn't want to perform it at the wedding, which could potentially take attention away from Lauren and Patrick.

Although it's a very rudimentary, syrupy, basic song, the sentiment of it, expressing my love for Lauren, comes through loud and clear. I hope that hearing the song, and dancing to it, is a memory she never forgets, especially since she inspired it.

*   *   *   *   *

A few months later, at the end of January 2019, Ed Melnick invited Amy and me to visit him and his husband, Barry, at their apartment in Puerto Rico. Although our children were long gone from the school system, we had remained very close friends with Ed. Amy would talk to him on the phone regularly, while I, too, would also touch base with him occasionally. The trip was fantastic. Ed and Barry lived in a sprawling four-bedroom duplex penthouse apartment right on the water. It was beautiful.

Years prior, I had shared with Ed my being in a twelve-step program, and he was fully familiar with twelve-step language. On that visit, I told Ed that I had a storyline for a musical focused on the subject of addiction. The working title of the show would be *We*, as the word *we* is the first word in the First Step for all twelve-step programs. "We admitted we were powerless over alcohol—that our lives had become unmanageable."

In the play, I found myself wanting to make the point that all the twelve-step programs are founded on the same twelve steps of AA. This is a truly amazing fact, largely unknown by most. So, whether it's Gamblers Anonymous, Cocaine Anonymous, Overeaters Anonymous, Sexaholics Anonymous, or Narcotics Anonymous, they all share the same steps.

The impetus for writing the play itself comes from my gratitude for the life that AA has allowed me to live, giving me inspiration to help others. As I have seen, the various twelve-step programs have saved countless lives, easing hardships. It is the gratitude for these programs that motivated me to write the play. Of course, with my passion for music, I knew that song would have to be an essential part of the storytelling mechanism. With that in mind, though I had an outline and a strong foundation for the storyline of the musical, I had put the entire thing on hold because I really didn't know *how* to write music or dialogue. I found myself discussing the idea again on the trip to Puerto Rico.

When Ed asked me about my progress on the play, I told him, "I'm stalled. I need someone who writes music and knows the twelve-step vernacular."

He looked up and said, "I have just the guy."

Enter Benjamin Hey! Ed had met Ben at a writing group and had later attended one of Ben's live performances. As Ed discovered, Ben was not only an accomplished singer but a songwriter too. In fact, he calls himself a "daily songwriter" because he literally writes one song a day. Just what I needed.

Just weeks before our trip to Puerto Rico, Barry and Ed had invited Ben down for a visit. By the time we got there, Ben's visit was still fresh in Ed's mind, which is why he immediately thought of introducing me when I was talking about my need for a songwriter. We initially met via text before later meeting in Manhattan upon my return. Ed would later say that the introduction to Ben was just meant to be. I agreed. I thought to myself, *In AA, on any given day, at any given moment, it is not unusual to hear someone say, "There are no coincidences."* I think that this connection to Ben was one of those examples. Like so many events in my life, sheer accident or coincidence seems to impact destiny. Was it all planned or accidental? As Tony Robbins often says, "Proximity is the messenger of fate."

Once we met up in New York, Ben and I immediately clicked when it came to music. We both had a wide range of music we liked, neither stuck on a genre or a time period. And although we do have some different preferences, we are both naturally curious and open to learning about music we have never heard before. As I learned, Ben was a self-taught pianist who understood song structure and studio production. In fact, Ben had given up his career as a top-level fitness instructor to immerse himself in his songwriting craft. He was creating quite a résumé of modeling and acting jobs as well. All in all, it seemed as if he was very organized and disciplined in his work. I learned a lot from him.

From the time I met Ben, we wrote approximately twenty songs for my musical about addiction. We were on a real roll until Covid hit, which sidetracked everything. By this point, we were hesitant to meet and distracted by the insanity of the times, the sickness and deaths of some of our closest friends. I lost two truly remarkable friends—Orlando and Arthur, the brothers-in-law of Taryn (Amy's maid of honor and my high school classmate). As I mentioned earlier, both Orlando and Arthur had been instrumental in kindly helping us when we tried experimental treatments for Greg. Orlando was simply one of the sweetest, most well-intended humans I've ever met. And Arthur was a *great* friend and human being. There he was caring for all his patients while being struck down himself by such a terrible disease. To this day, I think about them both all the time.

So, yes, Covid was a "distraction," to say the least, one that sidetracked the idea of making music. In addition, I faced other obstacles as I continued writing the play. In 2019, I knew that I had a solid foundation for the musical itself, good characters, and a storyline, but while I could create music, I could *not* write dialogue. I simply could not imagine the dialogue between characters required to evoke and string together the music and story of the play. The dialogue I wrote was stilted. I had to put the play on hold.

Instead, I started writing pop music with Ben, nonrelated to the play, intending to release our songs through my own production company, which I called John Beyer Music. I hired Ben to write the music, produce it, and perform it. So far, we have written a dozen songs in a variety of styles. Some are hip-hop and ballads, others more Broadway and R&B. Of the group, some are total collaborations, and others are predominantly written by me or Ben. You'd be surprised to know which one of us was more involved in a hip-hop creation and who was on the ballad. Yes, it's me who conceived and wrote most of the lyrics called "Ra-ta-tat-tat," a song about gun violence and a plea to end it.

Among our other songs: "Powerless," a very personal song, a slow ballad originally written for my play, all about alcoholism and addiction; "No Samples," a great R&B song largely written by Ben, probably the richest song we've released, one that Ben nails in performance; "Love You More," a song I wrote in which I enlisted my daughter too. She starts the song by softly saying, "I love you." I respond, "No, my dear, let me make it clear, I love you *more* . . ." Then the music bursts into a fun, upbeat, light-hearted pop song about love, inspired, of course, by Lauren and my beautiful granddaughter Harper.

In all our work, Ben is creative and brings focus, organization, and structure. I like to think of my input by quoting what Sinatra said about Stephen Sondheim's classic, "Send in the Clowns": "It's a lovely marriage of words and music." I often find myself guiding the message of the song to make it more succinct and emotional, giving it more meaning.

As of the writing of this book, Ben and I have fully produced and released seven songs, split between those performed by me and by him. For any reader interested in finding our music, you can search for each artist individually on Spotify, Apple Music, or YouTube, or you can go to www.JohnBeyerMusic.com and find them all there. We have over two million streams collectively and are very proud of that! But keep in mind it takes over seventy-five million streams on one song to get a gold record! Hey, ya' neva' know . . .

On a final "note," our entire family has gotten a kick out of my musical pursuits, so different from moving and storage. The love of music truly runs in our family. We all look forward to an annual family event, which is going into New York City to see a Broadway play or musical, a day filled with incredible excitement. Over the last several years, some of the shows we've seen are *Hamilton, Dear Evan Hansen, MJ*, and *Kimberly Akimbo*. I hope that one day we might all be attending the opening of *my* musical, *We*.

CHAPTER 12

UP AND DOWN AND OVER AND OUT

Each time if find myself
Flat on my face
I pick myself up and get back in the race . . .

—"THAT'S LIFE," DEAN KAY AND KELLY GORDON (1963)

BEGINNING IN December of 2020, a series of profound events began to occur that would forever alter my life for all my remaining days and change my outlook on life forever.

First, the good news . . .

One weekend in December of 2020, Lauren and Patrick came over to our house in Glen Head, where we had been living for twenty-eight years. Christmas was coming, so they walked into the kitchen and casually handed Amy and me an early gift to open.

When I pulled away the wrapping paper, inside was a Christmas ornament that read, "Our little present to be unwrapped 2021."

OMG! They were having a baby. Amy and I were ecstatic, over the moon about the idea of our little girl having a baby. That day I laughed and I cried as I hugged Lauren fiercely and I affectionately patted Patrick on the face. There's great video showing how out of control my emotions were at this moment. I'm happy to report we all laughed at my expense.

At this point, Lauren and Patrick had purchased a home in Port Washington, just blocks from Gregory's home. And because this house was under a full gut renovation, and because the lease on their previous apartment was up, they needed a place to live. So, they temporarily moved into our house in Glen Head. As soon as I learned they were buying a home in Port Washington near Greg, I told Amy I wanted to move closer to our children. I immediately started looking for a new home for us.

I found a beautiful house in Sands Point, a village located at the tip of the Cow Neck Peninsula in the town of North Hempstead, in Nassau County, on the North Shore of Long Island. Compared to the Glen Head house, which was 3,000 square feet, this new one was huge, over 6,500 square feet in all. It was quite a house, over twice as large as what we had in Glen Head, and it cost three times more than I had ever imagined spending! But I thought, *What the hell?* At this point, Amy and I were almost sixty, so I felt like, *This is it! Let's enjoy it.* So we made the move.

The house, which was only two years old, is set on two acres directly facing the Long Island Sound. It is incredible. It has the large master bedroom on the main floor, four bedrooms, five and a half bathrooms, expansive views of the water, high ceilings in every room, and a swimming pool too. The best part was that it was only two miles from Lauren's house and two and a half miles from Greg's. I looked at this house as a resort so the kids would want to come to visit. The proximity, being physically close, would make it easier for everyone in so many ways, including being emotionally closer as well.

Even though the house was essentially brand new, we did do some renovations once we bought it in order to make it ours.

At the same time, Lauren and Patrick's home had been under a complete gut renovation, so they had been living with us in Glen Head. When our new Sands Point house was ready, the four of us moved into it in early June of 2021. By this time, Lauren was very pregnant. For me, being so close to family and having a new home made it an extremely happy time. This was very different from what I experienced in my childhood. I remember thinking that in no other time in my life had I felt more like living one day at a time, an affirmation learned in AA. Indeed, you *could* live a little better. In every way imaginable, I was living proof of this. I felt that so very deeply. Needless to say, the anticipation of the baby was tremendously driving my sense of gratitude. It was a super exciting time.

After an unremarkable pregnancy, our new granddaughter, Harper Jane Bardsley, was born August 16, 2021, delivered by caesarian section.

I must say, with all objectivity, the baby was stunning. Harper had blonde hair and bright blue eyes. In fact, hers were the kind of vivid blue eyes that you immediately knew were staying blue, not just through the newborn period. She looked so much like her good-looking father, Patrick. Amy and I were overjoyed.

Harper was born during Covid, and visitors were not allowed in the hospital. Not even the grandparents. UUUGGHHHH!!!!

Now the challenging news. I say challenging (rather than bad news) because when you eventually come out on the other side of a crisis, you can learn and grow from it. As you read in the poem "Welcome to Holland," you never know what you're going to experience through a crisis. Good things can come out of it and create new outlooks and new perspectives.

Here was the challenge: Harper was born with a birthmark of sorts, a port wine stain on her skin, located on and above her right eye and on her forehead. And her right eye was also bulging.

Because Lauren had had a caesarian and was staying in the hospital for a few days, her doctors indicated that they were going to do some tests on Harper. Their fear was that she had a condition called Sturge-Weber syndrome (SWS), a rare vascular disorder characterized by the association of a facial birthmark called a port-wine birthmark, abnormal blood vessels in the brain, and eye abnormalities such as glaucoma. Like autism, this condition also has a wide spectrum of severity. When it's mild, the patient can live a perfectly normal life; but when it's severe, the life of the afflicted can include severe glaucoma, vision problems, neurological impairments, and seizures that can even result in being wheelchair-bound.

It took a few days for this information to unfold. Meanwhile, we couldn't actually see the baby because of the Covid restrictions. As for the baby's condition, Lauren and Patrick didn't want to worry us until they had conclusive information. On the day the baby was leaving the hospital, with the MRI results confirming a diagnosis of SWS, they finally told us about the problem. We were absolutely scared and heartbroken. The thought of our daughter having a child with special needs absolutely wrecked me. As for Lauren and Patrick, they seemed outwardly calm, perhaps either numb or just trying to be stoic. Of course, their joy of having a baby was now tempered by the reality and fear of this very serious diagnosis.

When Lauren and Harper came home a few days later, the immense joy we all felt was guarded, mixed with silent concern for this beautiful little baby. Lauren and Patrick handled her wonderfully, with tremendous natural parental intuition. Likewise, they handled their concern for Harper's condition with immense maturity, focus, and levelheadedness. Amy and I had to squash our sense of fear. In fact, at times, when we wanted to give advice or insist on second and third opinions or potential alternative treatments, we had to rigorously bite our tongues. This situation was traumatic for everyone. Yes, Harper's medical condition was bringing back all the pain of Greg's autism diagnosis, which had occurred at the time of his second birthday.

I was sick, consumed with worry about this. The thought of our daughter having a child with developmental issues was quietly driving me insane. It concerned me more than I even understood or knew at the time.

Like Lauren and Patrick, Amy and I also sprang into action—reading up on SWS, calling medical practitioners, and searching the internet, finding out whatever we could. Amy and I are aggressive action-takers, and Patrick and Lauren are connected, and we quickly managed to secure a very hard-to-get appointment with a renowned skin-laser physician less than one week after Harper was born. Amy and I were careful not to take charge. We were determined to be loving, caring, and supportive to Harper, Lauren, and Patrick as best we could.

On the day of this appointment, the doctor recommended a series of facial laser treatments. Although each of the treatments would last only a minute or two, it was excruciatingly painful to Harper, who was crying and screaming at the top of her lungs. Lauren and Patrick had to help pin Harper down during each of the treatments. Watching their baby suffer this way was an incredibly upsetting and draining experience for the two of them. After approximately ten grueling laser treatments and the passage of time, the eye bulge subsided and the marks on Harper's skin faded dramatically, almost completely disappearing.

Just weeks after the baby was born, while in the midst of these treatments, we were all sitting on the couch watching a football game over Labor Day weekend. At one point, Lauren started shivering, even though it wasn't cold in the house. She asked me if I had the A/C cranked up on high, which I did not. It turned out she had a fever. We thought it might be Covid, so she went to a nearby walk-in clinic to get checked. The doctor ruled out Covid but sensed that something wasn't right. Knowing that Lauren had recently had a caesarian, he sent her immediately to the emergency room at the local hospital, just blocks away.

It turned out that she had a severe, life-threatening infection. Her white blood cell count was through the roof. She was immediately put on Vancomycin, one of the most powerful antibiotics that exists. ACT scan showed that she had a huge pocket of puss lodged between her appendix and colon. If it had infiltrated the colon, we were told that she certainly could have died.

Lauren was fully committed to breastfeeding and was very successful at it during the first weeks. But suddenly, with her being hospitalized, she was separated from the baby and couldn't nurse her. We had to scramble to get the "right" organic formula as a substitute. We all took part in caring for Harper. Amy was a fantastic grandmother, Patrick a great dad, and I was there too, all of us filling in for the new mother who was suddenly incapacitated. After almost a week, Lauren finally came home. She was in considerable pain, with a drain attached to her abdomen. She remained on heavy doses of antibiotics for all of September and into October.

As we entered October, things seemed to be improving. Lauren was on the mend, and Harper hadn't had any seizures. The big renovation of their house was winding down, and they were soon going to be moving into their new home. Life was looking better, and it seemed as if we had gotten through the worst of it. Although we still had concerns for Harper and Lauren, both were definitely doing better.

One day that fall, while Amy and I were watching TV, she noticed my shirt oddly pulsating. "Honey, look, what the hell is going on?" My heart was jumping so wildly that you could literally see my shirt moving up and down. Over the years, because my father had had a few heart attacks, I had periodically seen my cardiologist. Over the previous few months, I had noticed that my heart was racing from time to time, but it always passed, so I didn't give it much attention. But now, I quickly made an appointment to see the doctor.

On the day of the visit, I was given a nuclear stress test that revealed a potential blockage in the artery of the heart. The doctor recommended a routine angiogram and told me that I might need one or two stents inserted via an angioplasty. I agreed to the procedure. A few days later, I went in for what was supposed to be a quick, simple outpatient procedure. But I wound up being in the hospital for days.

While in recovery, we discovered that during the angiogram I had had a stroke! A piece of plaque had broken off and gone behind my eye, which significantly impaired my vision. Trying to see with both eyes was dizzying because my right eye was no longer centered. Instead, it was positioned off on its own to the far right.

In addition, while still in recovery at the hospital I had overdosed on fentanyl, the sedative they had given me during the angiogram. Even though I was fully awake, my oxygen suddenly dropped dramatically. I was about to die. They administered Narcan to reverse the overdose. Here I was, sober for thirty-six years at the time, and I'm being given Narcan in a hospital after having suffered an overdose and a stroke! You can't make this stuff up.

Once the overdose was dealt with, I was admitted into the hospital for several days to understand and assess the damage done by the stroke. At this point, if I tried to see with both eyes it would cause projectile vomiting. I had to wear a patch over my right eye. I was incredibly upset. In addition, when I was ready to go home, I had to use a walker since my balance was now compromised. I hated the walker. I had to take the stairs one *step* at a time—another irony, me taking "the steps" one by one. Once I was home, I just sat there on the couch, unable to drive. Another irony—me, the Man on the Move, unable to move. It was maddening. I had just gone in for a routine angiogram and left the hospital having had a stroke and overdosed on fentanyl!

Despite my extreme frustration, little by little, my eye started to become centered again and the dizziness lessened. Gradually, after weeks, I didn't need the patch all the time, though my vision was still somewhat wonky. By Christmas I started to drive again, but only on local streets, not on the highway. I felt shaky and insecure and just wasn't ready yet.

By the beginning of 2022, things were again looking up again. Harper seemed fine, Lauren was now fully healed, and I was very much headed toward a 98 percent recovery. My vision was improving every day. I was going to be turning sixty-two in several weeks and I was looking forward to my birthday. I was starting the new year with a great sense of optimism, putting all the issues of the last several months behind us.

*　　*　　*　　*　　*

On February 4, 2022 (my sixty-second birthday), I got a call from Dr. Jia Li, my oncologist from Memorial Sloan Kettering. She was following up on my routine annual CT scan exam, which I had just taken, calling me with the results.

Four and a half years earlier, I had been diagnosed with stage 2A colon cancer, meaning that I had a two-inch tumor (fairly large), but the cancer had not spread to nearby tissue or to the lymph nodes. As it turned out, in the surgery that followed, the tumor in the colon was removed along with my appendix and thirteen inches of my colon. This all happened very quickly, and it didn't seem very scary at the time. Recovery was easy. The whole ordeal was manageable. Because the margins were clear, no chemo was required. In my mind (perhaps to protect myself from undue worry or fear) it felt very neatly taken care of— done, complete, let's move on. As the doctor said, "I believe we got it all." Recovery thereafter was pretty smooth, no real pain or discomfort. Over the next four years, I had routine colonoscopies and CT scans to make sure that, in fact, the doctor had gotten it all. They *didn't*.

Flash-forward: Dr. Li called me with results. "During your most recent CT scan, we discovered a three-by-three-inch tumor in your liver," she stated in an even tone. I sat there stunned . . . I had *no* symptoms other than unusual fatigue, which I had experienced for the last several weeks. "John, you should make an appointment with one of our surgeons as soon as possible to assess the possibility of surgically removing the tumor."

Although Memorial Sloan Kettering is known to be one of the premier hospitals in the US in treating cancer, they had nonetheless misdiagnosed my colon cancer, calling it stage 2A. Instead, I now had stage 4 metastatic colon cancer of the liver, an apparently common result of having colorectal cancer in the first place. I was stunned, shaken. Talk about wrecking your birthday. This was serious, and I was scared.

Before the doctor called me that day, my mind had been entirely on my storage business. At that time, we were being courted by multiple large self-storage companies who wanted to buy two of the three facilities we owned. I had originally wanted to sell only one of them, the smaller, less profitable one. But the company wanted to buy both or neither. But since it was my birthday, I had put all thoughts of business aside since Amy and I had plans to go to our favorite restaurant—Bryant and Cooper Steakhouse in Roslyn. We dined there over thirty years and always loved it.

I got the cancer call at 2:00 p.m. Dinner was planned for 7:00 p.m. I didn't want to ruin the night by telling Amy anything about the cancer call. So, I thought I'd at least wait to tell her until after we got home later. But while driving to the restaurant, I found myself saying, "We are going to sell both properties." I found myself thinking, *Clear up the work for her, take the money, and let her live a good life.*

The restaurant is one of those steak houses that has those brass name plates with customer names on the walls. When we walked into the restaurant, I spontaneously asked Joseph the maître d' (who was a fixture there) if we could have our names engraved on one of those brass nameplates.

"What's going on with you?" Amy chuckled. "First you weren't going to sell the warehouses, and now, after thirty years coming here, you want a nameplate?"

"Well," I said, "we're getting older, so perhaps it's time for both!"

Anyway, we had a great dinner. Even though it's known for being a steakhouse, they have an amazing, award-winning tuna steak dish, which I had. While I don't drink, Amy enjoyed her martinis and got pleasantly tipsy. That night she made quite an amusing birthday toast, worth repeating: "To you, John, happy birthday. I hope we celebrate your birthday here for the next twenty-five years—even if," she joked, "we are divorced." We both laughed, and I could not help thinking to myself, *From your mouth to God's ears.* (About the twenty-five years, not the divorce part.) But based on the earlier conversation with the doctor, twenty-five more years seemed very unlikely.

We drove home, and after walking inside, and I sat her down and told her the bad news. After the shock and tears and her peppering with many questions that I was unable to answer, we went to bed. Though she was trying to hide it, I could tell that she, too, was scared.

As Amy remembers it, "I knew something was wrong by the way John said he needed to talk to me about something. That was ominous. I was waiting to hear who had died. He was too calm for it to be anyone very close to us. I never expected him to say the cancer had returned, this time in his liver. I initially had trouble processing it. I was scared. I had questions. And he didn't have answers."

We didn't have the answers *yet* . . .

The next day was Amy and I at our best. We both sprang into action, calling my sisters and others, getting support and more information about the diagnosis and treatment for it. Our days were filled with doctor's appointments, conversations with family and friends, the search for an attorney so that we could update our wills—all while trying to continue life as normal. We went to the oncologist's office and asked a million questions, taking copious notes. We researched and found the surgeon we wanted. It was during this time that I decided to release the song "Powerless." Though I had been holding back release of this song for the play about addiction, I didn't know if that would ever come to be. Who knew how the surgery would turn out? So I decided to put the song out into the universe. I thought, *Maybe it'll help someone else through a crisis.* Or maybe I was releasing it because I was realizing that *I* was powerless at the time . . .

In advance of the surgery, Amy was becoming increasingly anxious and worried.

"As it got closer to the day of John's surgery," she says, "the seriousness of his condition started to hit me. There we were, working on our wills and decisions that needed to be made while I thought to myself, *What if . . .* I couldn't even finish the sentence. *How am I going to do this by myself?"*

On March 1, 2022, at Sloan Kettering in NYC, approximately four weeks after my diagnosis, I had surgery to remove the cancerous tumor. During the seven-hour operation, the doctors removed two-thirds of my liver. As I was later told, even though the tumor was considered large, I was fortunate that there was only *one* tumor and that it wasn't in a particularly complicated section of the liver. That is, it wasn't near where the liver was connected to another organ, which would have made the surgery much more difficult or even impossible. This made it operable. When I opened my eyes afterward, I was told the procedure was a success. The first night I remained in ICU to begin my recovery.

The next day I was a bit loopy, but conscious and able to talk with Amy, albeit in whispers. Amy retells the story of the day:

> As it turned out, the surgery went well—until it *didn't.* John wasn't bouncing back as expected, feeling more uncomfortable than anticipated. As the hospital was still operating under Covid protocols, only one registered visitor was allowed per day (not one at a time). Yet everyone wanted to go see John.
>
> So, two days after the surgery, John wanted the one visitor to be his best friend from high school, Bob Bellusci, who called me to say that John wasn't doing well. I asked Bob to put me on speakerphone as soon

as the doctor came back into the room. When I got him on the phone, I pleaded with him to find a way to get me into the hospital. Right afterward, I headed into the city. I remember waiting in the car outside Sloan Kettering, calling the doctor's office again and again to find out if I could be allowed in. Finally, someone met me at the hospital entrance and escorted me to the ICU.

Bob met me outside the room, took off his gown, mask, and slippers, and instructed me on the protocols. He said he would be waiting for me in the waiting room. I spent about an hour and a half with John. Then the doctors said I had to leave until a different doctor told me I could go back into the room. As I entered, John was really struggling. What the hell had happened in the three minutes I was gone?! I waved the doctor down and asked them to hurry. After some discussion among themselves, they turned to me and said, "We need to intubate him, hopefully for just a few days. His body needs to rest."

I have a very clear memory of my crash: Suddenly, I couldn't breathe. I mean I *really* couldn't breathe. I somehow communicated that to Amy and then the unit nurses were rushing in. With my respiration dropping and my blood oxygen level plummeting, the next thing I knew I was being rushed into the ICU, intubated, and put on a ventilator. The doctors and nurses were telling me

249

everything they were doing every step of the way, and I was completely aware of what was happening—all too aware.

"Just before they performed the procedure, they made me leave the room," recalls Amy. "Bob had stayed behind, just as he said he would, and I saw the shock and pain on his face as I told him about John's deteriorating condition. We sat there together, squeezing hands as we waited."

I was in incredible pain from the surgery, not breathing on my own, and I also had a high fever. But the doctor couldn't give me anything for the fever or the pain, as I had only one-third of a liver left and *that* was failing. So, in an effort to bring my fever down they covered me in bags of ice—everywhere. There was ice on top of me on my chest, under my arms, between my legs, under my neck, and in every fold of my body. I lost consciousness. To all, it appeared I was dying.

Amy was in shock:

Finally, we were brought into the room. Thankfully, John was at peace, no longer struggling to breathe, no pain on his face.

Although Bob wanted to drive me home while others offered to send a car for me, I turned everyone down. I needed to drive so I wouldn't think about what was happening. In the car, I conferenced in a call with John's two sisters. Meanwhile, the doctor called in, advising me that the next twenty-four to forty-eight hours would tell the story. When I got home,

Lauren was at the house waiting and stayed with me throughout the night. We didn't talk much. I had trouble sleeping and called the hospital a few times to find out if his fever had broken and to get updates on his latest liver numbers. I tried to get back to sleep but couldn't. I kept thinking, *Is he still alive?* Then I got up and started walking around the house, wondering, *What am I going to do in this house by myself? This was John's dream . . . not mine. Why is this happening?*

The hardest part of all this was going through it on my own. Sure, I had Lauren and Patrick, John's sisters, Bob, and our close friends. But throughout my entire adult life, John and I faced the toughest struggles together. We always got through them *together*. But now we were temporarily apart at the time I needed him the most. I was numb and so scared. I would just have to get through this one on my own.

Then, with no explanation, after about thirty-six hours of being on a ventilator, my fever broke, and my numbers improved. As Amy puts it, "A very small healthy part of John's remaining liver tissue had decided it wanted to live and stopped failing. The doctor had no explanation. He said he had never seen anyone fail so fast and had never seen anyone recover so quickly."

I suddenly regained consciousness and started breathing on my own. The tube was removed from my throat. As Amy tells everyone,

When I arrived at the hospital, John looked up at me and said, "I'm not going anywhere. I am a tough son-of-a-bitch."

I answered, "I know that. Just glad *you* know it too!"

But the long-term impact of John being on a ventilator has never quite left me. I didn't realize the effect it had on me until John needed to go for additional testing months later. Though the procedure was outpatient, he needed to wear a surgical gown and cap as he waited in the hospital bed for the procedure to begin. As I sat next to him waiting, my breathing increased and I almost had a panic attack. I believe it was PTSD. And it continues to happen every time I'm standing or sitting beside him during a medical test.

Recovery was hell. I was supposed to be in the hospital for five or six days, but I stayed for a total of twelve. Discouragingly, as I was being released, they wheeled me to the front door and then gave me a walker, my second walker in six months. I should have used it, but my macho pride prevented me from being sensible. Fortunately, I did not fall on the way to the car.

To this day, the surgeon and the medical team at Sloan remain perplexed as to why I suddenly failed so quickly, knocking on death's door, and then came back just thirty-six hours later. Perhaps it was the prayers of Sister Ann from Cormaria Retreat House, who told Amy, "I had the bums praying, the Jesuits

praying, the Jews praying, plus all the nuns!" Thank you, Sister
Ann Marino.

*   *   *   *   *

I left the hospital on March 13, surgery being just less than two
weeks prior. Though I refused to use the walker in my house, I
really could have used it that first week. I was weak, exhausted,
and had no appetite. I was also feeling quite depressed. My
body, mind, and spirit were in shock. I literally and figuratively
had taken quite a blow to the gut. Compounding all this was the
fact that I had no voice, as the intubation had damaged my vocal
cords. I could only whisper or gasp. I was instructed not to speak
at all or to speak as little as possible so as to speed up the healing
process of my throat.

All I could do was lie on the couch and watch TV. I didn't
have the strength or focus to read. Instead, I watched March
Madness college basketball all day long. It did reignite my passion
for the game. But not being able to speak was driving me crazy. It
frustrated the hell out of Amy when I would be sitting next to her
on the couch, texting her my thoughts while she was only a foot
or two away from me. It was maddening for both of us. I couldn't
help but think how appropriate it was that we were in the middle
of the March Madness season.

It took about a month after the surgery for me to begin to
speak again, ever so gently, in order to hold a conversation. When
you're sick, it's always good to have a goal. My immediate goal was

to make my nephew's wedding on April 1. I asked my doctors for some cortisone to give me energy and reduce pain, but because I was still growing my new liver back, they didn't want to give it to me. I managed to find some old Prednisone in my medicine cabinet and started taking it a few days prior to the rehearsal dinner. It helped. It gave me some strength, an appetite, and a bit of energy. That day at the wedding, my brother-in-law Steve sobbed when he saw me enter the room looking so pale and weak. All of my nieces and nephews and their spouses surrounded me and gave me huge hugs and kisses. I had made it to the wedding. I even got up to dance for a few minutes with my two sisters. When Cherie saw me struggling, she stopped it. "Take it easy, let's go sit down." True enough, I was drained for days after the event. But I'll never forget being surrounded by my family and witnessing and having so much love for my nephew and his wife.

After the surgery, I was still experiencing considerable pain, so I was allowed to take a painkiller, the highly addictive Oxycodone, but only one at night for sleep. But since it did nothing to relieve my pain, I took it only once. Also, I had experienced seeing too many people who had started up on oxy and then become addicted to it, graduating to heroin and ultimately dying of an overdose. So instead of taking the oxy, I was relegated to only six Tylenols a day. However, I was happy when the doctor told me that I was growing a new liver. That was a ray of hope.

Even though I was still weak from everything that had happened, my doctor made me begin chemo just three weeks after the surgery.

Let me start by saying that chemo is devastating. There are dozens of ways it might affect you, from fatigue and constipation or diarrhea to hair loss, nausea, and mood changes. But it's not the same for everyone. Some people get few side effects or even none at all. I thought I was going to "macho through it" for the next six months. Bullshit. It's devastating. It knocks you on your ass and it ages you.

For starters, I had sixty large metal staples (stitches) in my abdomen. Some were from a chemo pump they installed subcutaneously near my belly button. This pump was key, as I was treated with two different chemotherapies. One was through a port in my shoulder for what is referred to as systemic chemo; the other was through the pump, which leads directly to the liver. This chemo delivers up to four hundred times the potency of the full-body chemo. I refer to it as "the nuclear weapon." I did this regimen for months. Needless to say, taking these chemo treatments *greatly* weakens your immune system.

Over the next few months, I experienced a number of health emergencies.

First, I got E. coli, a serious bacterial infection. You and I could have eaten the same salad containing the same bacteria, but because of my compromised immune system I got very sick and spent a night in the hospital. Then, after two years of managing *not* to get Covid, I finally got it. I got sick the day my music collaborator Benjamin Hey! was performing the song we had written ("Ra-ta-tat-tat") at Spotify headquarters. That day, I was so weak that I didn't think I was going to be able to drive home from the city. I thought I was going into the hospital again. I was vividly reminded of my two friends, Arthur and Orlando, whom I had lost to Covid. My doctor immediately put me on Paxlovid. After thirty-six hours, I started to feel a little better and my fever broke. But for two weeks, I lost my ability to taste food.

But then the third crisis came along, which really knocked me out. That's when I got rotavirus, a serious infection that causes a high fever, chills, headache, and extreme diarrhea. The pain was awful, excruciating. It's like someone is stabbing you very slowly in the stomach with a long dagger, the pain going on and on, as if the dagger is slowly being inserted into your abdomen and pulled back out, again and again.

I was immediately admitted to a local hospital and put on intravenous fluids, painkillers, and antibiotics for days. The stomach issues were serious, and I thought it would never get under control. I couldn't eat. I didn't even want to eat, and I certainly couldn't sleep. At this point, I was so beaten up and so discouraged that I was a mess—exhausted, entirely depleted. I started to question whether the chemo was worth it.

These three events happened from May through the end of July. My chemo regimen was scheduled to end at the end of September, and I was still clinging to that. Even though you want the poison to kill any possible remaining cancer cells, I couldn't wait for it to be over. I so badly wanted it to be over.

Chemo ended at the end of September, but the pump remains inside of me to this day, as the statistics show that I have a 70 percent chance of cancer coming back. The pump is there in the event it does. You don't remove the pump, because once you do, it cannot be put back in. It's a "one and done" type of application. I plan on keeping the pump in for about five years. I am *not* giving up the nuclear weapon too soon. The pump does need routine maintenance. And I do have to visit MSK every two or three weeks. The protocol is that I get a CT scan *every* ninety days to check for any new cancer growths. So far, so good.

*   *   *   *   *

Through this entire ordeal, Amy and I tried to maintain our normal way of life.

One night while out to dinner with Bob Bellusci and his wife, Margi, they mentioned a best-selling book they had read called *The Tender Bar*, a memoir by J. R. Moehringer. Bob, who knew me well from my days tending bar, gave me a knowing look that only a best friend can. It conveyed his sentiment that I would love the book and should read it. As I would discover, it's all about the trials and tribulations of a boy growing up on Long Island with an absentee father and seeking out father figures among the patrons at his uncle's bar. (It became a movie directed by George Clooney and starring Ben Affleck.) The parallels between that book and my own life were uncanny and hit me hard. The real kicker was that the bar in the book is located in Manhasset, just a few miles from my house. Though I never drank there, I was immediately compelled to read the book at Bob's behest.

The story was very moving to me, but more than that, it was incredibly close to my own story. The main character's father is not around, the drinking, the well-described bar scenes, and the concept of a child parenting his mother. There was one particular section about the author waiting for his father to take him to a baseball game at Shea Stadium. "I was ready at four-thirty. Sitting on the stoop, wearing my Mets cap, slugging my fist into the pockets of my new Dave Cash mitt. I peered at every car that approached the house." Just like me.

He waited until 9:00 pm, but his father never appeared. Later that night, the boy's mother comforted him. "She walked quickly toward me and I wrapped my arm around hers, startled by how much I loved her and how intensely I needed her. As I held my mother, clung to her, cried against her legs, it struck me that she was all I had, and if I didn't take good care of her, I'd be lost."[1] But in my case, my mother couldn't comfort me. She was too lost in herself.

When I read those pages about this kid waiting and waiting for his father, I started to sob. In fact, I had to put the book down for a couple of weeks to consider if I was ever going to be able to pick it up again. That story about his dad mirrored the absolutely most painful part of my life—the desertion of my father and my desperate need to have him in my life. Waiting endlessly for a parent who never shows up is a heart-wrenching experience that left an indelible mark on my soul. I swore to

---

1 J. R. Moehringer, *The Tender Bar: A Memoir* (Hyperion, 2006).

God that I would have a better relationship with my son, but God had other plans.

While I was reading the book, I would repeatedly mention it to Lauren and Patrick because I was enjoying it so much. One day they stopped over and told me they found themselves thinking about my excitement with this book and said I should write my *own* book, a memoir about growing up in LeFrak City, about my own struggles as a child with alcoholic parents, and my success in the moving and storage business. At first, I thought she was kidding. But then one day, I can remember Lauren cornering me in the kitchen in a warm yet forceful way, saying, "Dad, you should do it. You have quite a story to tell. It's inspiring."

Lauren is smart and she was serious about it. I think she was also worried about my health and how close I had come to dying. She thought that since I had been so seriously ill, maybe writing a book should be added to my bucket list—which had already included singing, composing music, recording, and producing a play. Just as Lauren had inspired me to write a song for her wedding, I was once again being inspired by her to write a book. I am so grateful to her.

But I remained conflicted. It felt so self-indulgent and lacking in humility to write an entire book about myself—a bit egotistical to reveal my entire life, far from what I learned in Alcoholics Anonymous about humility and anonymity. But Lauren convinced me otherwise, saying that writing a book would inspire others and demonstrate what can be achieved one day at a time, by power of example.

As of this date, my play, *We*, the full-blown homage to the twelve steps of Alcoholics Anonymous, is not yet finished. While I understand very well that AA is a program of attraction, not promotion, the program can and ought to be celebrated. Another slogan in the program is that in order to "keep it" (your sobriety), "you have to give it away." So perhaps one way of doing that is to bring the message and the principles of the program into print and into theater.

As I considered whether or not to write a book, I also thought about my granddaughter, Harper (and possibly her future siblings), one day reading the story of my life. The book will hopefully give her a sense of who her grandfather was, what he did, and how he lived. I hope it guides her far beyond any legal papers directing her how to handle her financial legacy, one left for her benefit with the responsibility of managing it correctly.

Yes, living one day at a time, working very hard, and taking some unbelievable risks made me very successful in the traditional sense of making money and having material things. But the story, as you've seen, is about a lot more than that. More importantly, it's about love and creating a family. It's about surviving every twist and turn that fate throws at you. It's about staying strong when you're beaten down or sick, when you lose a friend or a family member, when you're afflicted with a disease that you rise to beat. All this has nothing to do with material success. This journey has proven to me that having success is only a small part of life.

I hope that my experience, strength, and hope will serve

as inspiration for anyone who is suffering from addiction of any kind, for anyone suffering an illness or a family crisis or any kind of challenge that tests their mettle. I know many people have suffered far more difficulties and worse obstacles than I have, but I do hope that reading my story helps someone, somehow.

Anyone who knows me knows that I love inspirational quotes. I have them all over my office. This is one of my favorites:

To know even one life has breathed easier
because you have lived. This is to have succeeded.
—Ralph Waldo Emerson

Absolutely true for me. I have found that the most rewarding thing in life is helping someone else—helping someone each day to just, well, *Live a Little Better*. I mean, after all, isn't that what we all really want?

AFTERWORD

As I am writing the final pages of this book, it feels like finishing one of my moving jobs. I've traveled from Point A, starting with a blank page, to Point B, a printed book. So, the last "box" has come off the "truck." The job is done here. But no doubt the moves are not finished; there will be many more "moves" to make.

As I look into the future, I find myself filled with optimism and immense gratitude for all that I have in my life—starting with my wife, Amy; our two children, Lauren and Greg; our son-in-law, Patrick; and, of course, our adorable granddaughter, Harper.

Regarding gratitude, given all the medical challenges I recently faced, I am hugely grateful for my physical health, which continues to be good. I am fortunate to have doctors who have literally saved my life and allowed me to continue *moving* forward—working and developing real estate, creating and recording music, and developing my musical, with a working title, *We*. When I reflect on all of it, I take pride in knowing that

I worked hard to allow myself and my family to *live a little better*, and I want that for others.

To that end, Amy and I have established the Beyer Family foundation, dedicated to helping families who face some of the challenges that we have known. First, our mission is to provide funding to organizations that support people on the autism spectrum. This, of course, includes Spectrum Designs of Port Washington, New York, the business cofounded by my son-in-law Patrick. It's a custom apparel and promotional products business with a social mission—to create meaningful and inclusive employment and vocational training opportunities for people in a neurodiverse world. More than 50 percent of the workforce at the company is on the autism spectrum, including my son, Gregory. As a nonprofit, 100 percent of sales from every order go toward the ongoing expansion and advancement of hiring and retaining an inclusive and integrated culture.

The foundation is also committed to serving people who are recovering from alcohol and drug addiction. Among the institutions that serve the needs of this recovering population is the Cormaria Retreat House, which the foundation will support.

We would also like to see the foundation evolve into helping those afflicted with seizure disorders like Sturge-Weber syndrome (SWS).

In addition, I would love our trust to create a mechanism whereby we teach financial literacy to those who aren't educated about money itself. Over the years, my relationship with money evolved. I now have an appreciation and understanding of the function of money that is very different than the teenage boy who had baseball cards in his shoes. With age, I appreciate the correlation between hard work and earning money and knowing how to use the money to make it work *for you*. I want the trust to fund education on this subject.

As you can see, our mission to help others has been inspired and driven by the experiences I've had as a recovering alcoholic, the father of an autistic son, and the grandfather of a girl impacted by Sturge-Weber. What I've come to learn about life is that helping others is the most rewarding thing you can do. I'm reminded of one of my favorite songs ever, "Alfie" by Hal David and Burt Bacharach. I don't know if I ever figured out what life was all about, but I do know it is important to always give more than you take and to always be kind.

ACKNOWLEDGMENTS

FIRST, AND CERTAINLY foremost, I want to thank Amy, my partner in every sense of the word, who, as I said in the dedication, makes everything possible. Amy has always given me the room to explore and live my dreams. But much more than that, she has tirelessly supported the pursuit of these dreams with an obsessive work ethic and commitment parallel to none. She is the bedrock of our family, a constant support in every way, and she contributed to this book immensely.

To my daughter, Lauren, who, together with Patrick, inspired me to pursue my late-in-life music career and the creative activity of writing this book. At first, I hesitated to tackle such a project, but Lauren persisted in her encouragement. This got done because of her insistence.

For my son, Gregory, who motivated me so much throughout my life as I watched him work as hard as he did. In fact, he has worked harder than anyone I know to become the best he can be. Though challenging at times, he set us on a journey in life that led us to fantastic relationships and experiences. I want to thank all of those who have worked with Greg and supported him.

I want to thank my dad, who I think of so often. The success he had as a photographer and entrepreneur in his early years inspired me to pursue my own business career, and perhaps I inherited the business gene from him.

I can never be thankful enough for my mom, who gave me the gift and love for music, spending endless hours with me listening and singing. Though my mother endured many hardships, she always demonstrated an example of sympathy and empathy for others.

To my sisters, Denise and Cherie, for being parents to me at a time when they were just kids themselves. They guided me through some tough times, providing a net beneath me, supporting me no matter what. The three of us always shared a loving and caring relationship, wanting the best for one another.

I also want to mention the incredible family support system I am fortunate to have, including my nieces and nephews and their spouses, all of whom I love so much. There's Jamie, Ashley and Steven, Dustin and Gina, Russell and Sarah, and Elizabeth and Marco.

A special thanks goes to my friend Lisa Golden, who also just happens to be my attorney. She has always guided me through every business transaction as if it were her own. After one particular closing, I got a call from an attorney "from the other

ACKNOWLEDGMENTS

side" saying he had "never seen an attorney work so hard for their client." That's Lisa! I cherish Lisa and her three magnificent daughters, Rachel, Lindsey, and Alana, and want to thank them for giving me so much of her time and bandwidth.

As far as the production of this book is concerned, I must thank my writing collaborator, *New York Times* bestselling author Glenn Plaskin, who has brought his touch to this book.

I am also grateful to the dozens of people who I may have failed to mention or incorporate into the book. This does not mean that I care about you less, so please do not feel forgotten or slighted at my stream of consciousness and thought process. You all had a definitive role in altering the direction of my life.

Last and certainly not least, I want to thank all of my AA friends—those from my home AA groups such as Bayside Hills, Douglaston Fresh Start, Little Neck, and now the Early Cup of Sobriety in Manhasset. I cherish, and take with me every day, the wisdom of every one of your shares.

Thank you all for showing me how to live a life beyond my wildest dreams, one day at a time.